D0908070

Library Services for Online Patrons

LIBRARY SERVICES FOR ONLINE PATRONS

A Manual for Facilitating Access, Learning, and Engagement

Joelle E. Pitts, Laura Bonella, Jason M. Coleman, and Adam Wathen, Editors

LIBRARIES UNLIMITED®
An Imprint of ABC-CLIO, LLC
Santa Barbara, California • Denver, Colorado

Library of Congress Cataloging-in-Publication Data

Names: Pitts, Joelle, editor.
Title: Library services for online patrons : a manual for facilitating access, learning, and engagement / Joelle E. Pitts, Laura Bonella, Jason M. Coleman, and Adam Wathen, editors.
Description: Santa Barbara, California : Libraries Unlimited, 2019. | Includes bibliographical references and index.
Identifiers: LCCN 2019026116 (print) | LCCN 2019026117 (ebook) | ISBN 9781440859526 (hardback) | ISBN 9781440859533 (ebook)
Subjects: LCSH: Library orientation—Web-based instruction. | Information literacy—Web-based instruction. | Online library catalogs—User education. | Online information services. | Reference services (Libraries)—Information technology.
Classification: LCC Z711.2 .L336 2019 (print) | LCC Z711.2 (ebook) | DDC 025.5/6—dc23
LC record available at https://lccn.loc.gov/2019026116
LC ebook record available at https://lccn.loc.gov/2019026117

ISBN: 978-1-4408-5952-6 (paperback)
      978-1-4408-5953-3 (ebook)

23 22 21 20 19   1 2 3 4 5

This book is also available as an eBook.

Libraries Unlimited
An Imprint of ABC-CLIO, LLC

ABC-CLIO, LLC
147 Castilian Drive
Santa Barbara, California 93117
www.abc-clio.com

This book is printed on acid-free paper (∞)

Manufactured in the United States of America

Contents

Introduction

Since the advent of the Internet in the mid-1990s, the role and value of library services and resources has been brought into question. Discussions around relevancy, technological aptitude, and the need to serve an increasingly online user base have been front and center at library conferences and other professional gatherings for more than two decades. Yet, libraries are still here, largely because they have found ways to serve their patrons in the digital age. They are not only relevant but are also necessary as information is proliferated at exponential rates.

There are few agreed-upon or official guidelines for serving online library users, and those that exist shift frequently as technology progresses and users adapt. This book is intended to be a manual for librarians who work with users learning, studying, connecting, and researching online. Though public services librarians have the most obvious interaction with these users, this book will also be helpful to other staff who manage electronic access and services. We focus on ways to build library services and resources using the principles of universal design, as well as how to cater to the specific needs of online users. We also address how to effectively reach out and market to the online population, and how to collaborate with organizational stakeholders who work directly with or for them. As a result, librarians who work with online users will have a practical blueprint to follow in implementing or improving their services and marketing.

This manual offers 10 chapters that each address an aspect of online librarianship. The first three provide a foundation for those that follow. Chapter 1 provides points of consideration, tactics, and useful resources for taking stock of your library through the online services lens. Chapter 2 further builds on your capacity to set realistic goals to serve or better accommodate your online users. Chapter 3 relates to inclusive design, or the intentional consideration of users with a variety of abilities and circumstances.

Chapters 4 through 6 offer an in-depth treatment of three cornerstones of public services for online users: reference, instruction, and embedded librarianship.

Chapters 7 through 9 each focus on aspects of online user service that are often considered later in the process, if at all, but remain vital components of holistic service to this population. Chapter 7 considers the kinds of outreach and relationship building that allow an organization to augment their services and resources and make them more robust. Chapter 8 provides a deep dive into marketing to online users. Chapter 9 examines how librarians can advocate for their online users especially with regard to access and provides a template for planning.

Chapter 10 describes how public library service to online patrons differs from the academic services described in previous chapters. Even though many of the considerations from previous chapters are applicable to public libraries, in many ways public libraries need a separate treatment because they deal with a different set of goals, tools, and patrons than academic libraries. Chapter 10 provides a discussion of public library practices in discovery, content, and programming for online users.

Each chapter in this volume is written by a librarian with in-depth practical expertise in serving online users. The chapters are also augmented with practical case studies from a variety of libraries. Each area could be (or in many cases already is) an entire volume in itself. This manual, therefore, is not meant to examine every facet and angle of online librarianship in detail. Rather, it is aimed at providing a practical, cohesive starting point for librarians hoping to have a broader and more holistic view of how to serve online users.

Throughout the book, we have been very careful in our use of the words *online* and *distance*. Although some librarians use those terms interchangeably, we do not. For us, the word *online* refers to resources and services that are accessed or delivered through the Internet. In the context of library users, *online* means those users who are interacting with the library through the Internet. The term *online* refers to the mode of access rather than the location of access. Indeed, many online users are situated in physical library buildings. The term *distance*, in contrast, refers to locations that are geographically separated from our library buildings. In the context of users, the word *distance* refers to individuals who are unable to, or prefer not to, visit our physical library locations.

CHAPTER ONE

Taking Stock of Your Library

Stefanie Buck

Introduction

When you work with online or distance patrons, you may find that you are full of ideas about how to serve them, but before you dive in and start creating online tutorials and services, it is best to take a step back and take stock of the situation. Taking stock means getting to know what resources are available to you, understanding policies and procedures, identifying what services are available to online learners, and knowing who your partners are. In this chapter, we will look at some of the questions you should ask in order to gain a better understanding of your situation. We will look at partners and stakeholders, tools and technology, collections, and policies. Some of these topics, such as conducting a needs assessment of your population, will be covered in more depth in later chapters. Because each situation is different, this chapter is made up in large part of questions to ask so that you have a good understanding of your environment. The answers to these questions will help you develop your plan for what you want to accomplish.

While there may be few librarians in your organization who focus on online patrons, chances are there are other librarians in your state or region who would be willing to share what has and has not worked for them. One good place to begin is by reading about the experiences of others. Some of their situations may provide guidance for your work. A few articles listed in the References to help you get started include Cannady, Fagerheim, Williams, and Steiner's *Diving into Distance Learning Librarianship: Tips and Advice for New and Seasoned Professionals* (2013); Corbett and Brown's *The Roles That Librarians and Libraries Play in Distance Education Settings* (2015); Holloway's *Outreach to Distance Students: A Case Study of a New Distance Librarian* (2011); Huwiler's *Library Services for Distance*

Students: Opportunities and Challenges (2015); and Marcum's *Embracing Change: Adapting and Evolving Your Distance Learning Library Services to Meet the New ACRL Distance Learning Library Services Standards* (2016).

Guiding Documents

In addition to the policies and procedures of your library and institution (more on that later), there are some external documents with which you will want to be familiar because these are guiding documents for you and your institution when it comes to evaluating and assessing your work.

Read the Standards!

The *Standards for Distance Learning Library Services* (2016) created by the Distance Learning Section of the Association of College and Research Libraries (ACRL), a division of the American Library Association (ALA), is a guiding document for academic libraries regarding services to online learners (Hebert, 2016; Wharton, 2017). The *Standards* define the expectations of a university library regarding services to online/distance learners, although other types of libraries serving online users can also benefit from the *Standards*' recommendations. The *Standards* cover important things to consider including:

1. Whom should online patrons contact if they need help?
2. What research and reference services does the organization provide? What should it provide?
3. What kinds of online resources are available? What should be made available?
4. What document and book delivery services are available? Do these meet the users' needs?
5. How can you assess your library's services to online patrons?

The *Standards* are also a tool to help you if you need to argue for more resources or a change in policies that will better serve your population. While not a binding document, it does represent the level of service endorsed professionally by ACRL. The latest version of the *Standards* is available online.

In addition to the *Standards for Distance Learning Library Services*, you may want to consult other relevant standards or guidelines. For example, if you serve patrons enrolled in an online nursing program, ALA's *Information Literacy Competency Standards for Nursing* (2013) would also be very important to your work. The complete list of ALA guidelines, standards, and frameworks is available at http://www.ala.org/tools/guidelines/standardsguidelines.

Strategic Plans

If your library has a strategic plan, and hopefully it does, where does the work you do fit in? Are there goals that the library wants to accomplish, and where does your job fit into these? If there is no strategic plan, ask for any planning or goal documents the library has produced so you can get a sense of the direction of the library. Some universities have strategic plans to help them decide where to focus their resources. While online learning may not appear explicitly in the plan, there will be important information here about what the university values and where the university wants to position itself. As you read these documents, ask yourself where distance and online learning fits.

Know the Accreditation Requirements for Your Institution

University libraries are an essential component of the accreditation and reaccreditation process. Each college and university in the United States must go through a regular review process to ensure that it "maintains standards requisite for its graduates to gain admission to other reputable institutions of higher learning or to achieve credentials for professional practice" (U.S. Department of Education, Office of Postsecondary Education, n.d.). There are regional as well as national and specialized accrediting agencies (https://ope.ed.gov/accreditation/agencies.aspx). When it comes to judging how well a library serves its students, the accreditation guidelines may provide a basic measure or requirement. Your institution will likely need regional accreditation but, if you have an extensive online learning program, may also need accreditation from the Distance Education Accrediting Commission. A specialized accrediting body must accredit some departments or programs. For example, if you have an online nursing program, the college will likely require accreditation from the Commission on Collegiate Nursing Education. You should know how the accrediting body defines distance and online learning and what the requirements of service are. These requirements may not be as specific as the *Standards* regarding library services, but you may be asked to document them.

Who Are You?

Understand Your Position

You may be inheriting a position, or your position may be entirely new. You may be a newly minted librarian or a seasoned veteran who is moving into a distance or online learning library position. The position may have been empty for a while or may have been recently reconfigured. If the position is new, you may not have a lot of guidance about the role; the expectation may be that you define it yourself. There are many different service models for serving online learners. You may not even have the title of distance or online librarian but may have these responsibilities in your position description. In some cases, there are teams serving online students, but in many cases, it is a rather solitary state. You may be at a regional or satellite campus, or you may be located in the main library. In any case, it is important to have a good understanding of the current situation and scope of the work that you are taking on.

Questions to consider:

- How is your role different from that of other librarians?
- How does your role integrate with the other librarians?
- How are you expected to interact with subject or liaison librarians?
- How are subject or liaison librarians expected to interact with you?
- How will you interact with other departments or services (e.g., interlibrary loan)?

Every distance or online position is unique and has its own set of challenges. To start with, you may need to get a better sense of how your position fits into the bigger library structure. One issue many online learning librarians have to deal with is ambiguity in terms of their position's relationship to that of the subject or liaison librarians. As the lines between online and distance become blurred, it may be necessary to have some conversations about where the boundaries are, and this may require some negotiations with your colleagues. While it is very helpful to know where the lines are and what the expectations are, expect to be flexible.

Get to Know Your Department and Colleagues

Once you have a better idea of your position and how it fits into the bigger picture, you will want to find out what your colleagues know about online learning at your institution, what services they may already provide, how the services are marketed, and what has or has not been working. Some interviews with your fellow librarians can be very useful here.

Take Stock of Your Own Skillset

What professional development opportunities are there for you? What support is there? What do you need to learn? As you get to know the expectations of the job, you may find that there are things you need to learn to do your job well. There are, fortunately, many local and national opportunities for you to gain additional skillsets and proficiencies. Some skillsets and proficiencies that are often required of distance or online learning librarians include (Tang, 2013):

- Online learning pedagogy
- Tutorial creation
- Web design
- Marketing and outreach
- Using learning management systems (LMS)
- Webinar or videoconferencing
- Subject knowledge
- Collection development
- Research skills

There are many ways to build up your skillset. Find out what kind of support is available for professional development, such as travel to conferences or continuing education. Some institutions have small grants or funding opportunities. Here are a few additional strategies:

- Get a subscription to the *Journal of Library and Information Services in Distance Learning* (Taylor & Francis)
- Get involved with ACRL's Distance Learning Section or a regional library association
- Find a mentor
- Attend the Distance Library Services conference

More suggestions for resources are in the Appendix.

Policies and Procedures

Learn the Policies: Library and Institution

Many libraries have specific practices regarding services to online learners, but these may not always be well documented or well known to your users. Some of these are university based. For example, one of the more tricky issues is how distance or online patrons are defined at your institution or library.

- Are they coded by the registrar? If so, how? How does this data get to the library?
- Do they have to be enrolled in a certain number of credits online to be considered distance or online?

There may be institutional policies that limit how you can contact online patrons.

- Can you send out blanket e-mails to all online patrons? If not, with whom can you work to communicate with patrons?
- Can you be integrated into the LMS?
- What permissions do you need to access student data? For example, do you need to go through training on the Family Educational Rights and Privacy Act of 1974?

Other issues are related more specifically to library policies. Because so many resources are now available online, online and distance learners have access to many more resources than in the past. However, print materials are still a little more challenging.

- Is there a geographical restriction for who is considered online or distance? For example, many libraries will only mail books outside a certain radius.
- Who pays for shipping and mailing of physical materials?
- Are there restrictions about what the library will or will not send?
- Where are these policies documented?

While policies are generally put in place to help regulate access, it is also possible that some of the policies are dated or no longer valid. Do the current policies limit, restrict, or present any unnecessary barriers? The less guesswork an online patron has to do about how and where to get resources or help, the better.

Stakeholders and Partners

Another challenge often faced by online learning librarians is that the structure of responsibility for online education may vary. In some cases, there will be a central unit managing online education; in others, it will be a distributed model. This can make it more challenging to identify all your partners and stakeholders. It is important to discover who is involved or has a stake in online education at your institution. Think broadly.

Stakeholders

- The department that manages online learning (if there is one)
- Departments/colleges with online programs
- Students
- Faculty and instructors
- Support services like tutoring or academic advising

Partners

- Library departments such as circulation, collections, interlibrary loan, and course reserves.
- Computer/technology support staff.
- The department that manages online learning (if there is one).
- Departments/colleges with online programs.
- Faculty (especially those who are interested in teaching online or already active online).
- College advisors are an often-overlooked resource, but they maintain very close contact with their students and can be very helpful in getting the word out about the library.
- LMS managers may be able to help you with issues such as automating the integration of library resources into the LMS, adding you to online courses and adding the library into the LMS course template.
- The registrar usually manages how students are identified as online or distance in the university system.

What Data Is Already Available to You?

One key element to being a successful online education librarian is that you get to know your users. This does not just include your students but also the instructors and other groups that support online learning. Just about every librarian who has taken this type of job has discovered the need to do some data gathering about their users, those users' needs, and how well they are served. You will want to do this at some point, too, but before you do, take some time to find out what data already exists. Given that your students as well as some of your instructors are off-campus, reaching them can be tricky (more on that in another chapter). However, it is likely that some data has already been gathered by either the library or other departments or units on campus.

Questions to consider:

- Who are the online learners, instructors, and support staff?
- Who offers/supports the online and distance programs?
- What data are they currently gathering?
- How can you get access to it?
- If there is a department that manages online or distance education, what data can it share with you?
- What data-gathering options are available?

If there was a predecessor in your position, see if you can find annual reports, surveys, or other data they may have gathered. Tap into what departments or colleges are gathering already so you do not need to duplicate any efforts. You do not necessarily need to have individual names; aggregate data is often enough to give you a good picture. This is also an opportunity for you to find out if you can insert some questions about the library into a preexisting survey. For example, the organization or individual departments may give an exit survey to graduating students. This could be an opportunity to add a question or two about library usage and perceptions of the library.

The kind of data you may be able to find will vary and may be limited based on the policies of the institutions. Some examples of data are:

- Student demographics: age, location, status, courses they are taking.
- Instructor data: status, title, location.
- Course data: who is teaching these courses, and what is the level of courses?
- Tutorials or learning module usage.
- Website usage: If there is a website for online learners, what usage data is being gathered? How is it available?
- Surveys done by online or distance education programs or departments.
- Information literacy attainment: Has anyone done any evaluation of online learners' information literacy skills?

Case Study: Developing a Needs Assessment Survey for Online Users

Erin McArthur, MLIS, Online Learning Librarian
Joe Pirillo, MLIS, MEd, Information Literacy/Online Learning Librarian
Polk Library, University of Wisconsin-Oshkosh

At Polk Library at the University of Wisconsin-Oshkosh, we are committed to implementing flexible information instruction programs that improve student information literacy and critical thinking skills. This commitment includes developing proactive support for online students and faculty. While our online learning services provided information literacy instruction in a variety of formats and venues online, we knew we could do better at proactively identifying our users' needs. None of the recent LibQUAL+ surveys our library conducted had differentiated between students in traditional on-campus programs and online users. Also, we had never conducted a library survey that sought input from both online students and instructors. In order to set new goals for our online learning services, we knew we needed to assess the current needs of all our online users.

We decided to create a simple needs assessment survey that would be adapted to both students and faculty. We needed a survey tool that was simple and cost effective, but one that could also accommodate the necessary number of responses. We chose Google Forms. Since our institution also uses Google Apps for Education, we were already familiar with the tool and it seemed like a good fit for our project. Unlike other alternatives such as SurveyMonkey, Google Forms allowed us to survey a larger population at no cost.

In developing questions for our survey, we reviewed the literature for best practices and examples of online library services needs assessments conducted at various academic institutions (Block, 2008; Buck, 2011; Jerabek, McMain, & Van Roekel, 2002; Lowe, Booth, & Savova, 2014; McLean & Dew, 2004). We also consulted ACRL's *Framework for Information Literacy for Higher Education* (American Library Association, 2015) when developing our questions on information literacy skills. We committed ourselves to only asking truly necessary questions that would result in specific action items. This meant disregarding potential questions that might be interesting but served little use except satisfying our curiosity. We chose 10 questions for both surveys that fell under four general categories:

- Who they were, and which departments they were from;
- Their history with our services, how they learned of those services and how we could better promote services to them in the future;
- Their perceived level of confidence in exercising critical information literacy skills, or how they perceived their students' ability to exercise these skills; and lastly,
- The key barriers they had experienced when using our services or resources.

Due to the somewhat fractured nature of online programs on our campus, we did not have access to a master list of students enrolled in online degree programs. In fact, we had difficulty even identifying all the different online degree programs. We eventually identified 13 online degree programs, 6 undergraduate-level and 7 graduate-level, and reached out to the program assistants for help disseminating our survey. In most cases, the program assistants provided us with a list of their students' and instructors' e-mail addresses, so we could contact them directly; a few programs preferred to contact students and instructors on our behalf. While we would have preferred that all departments shared their lists with us, we were grateful to have the cooperation of the programs in any capacity. Each surveyed group received an initial e-mail announcing the survey and two reminder messages.

To increase our response rate, we offered Amazon gift cards (three $25 cards for students; one $50 card for instructors) as incentives for completing the survey. We initially encountered some pushback from our administration, due to our university's policy that only gift cards to the campus bookstore can be given as prizes. We submitted a justification explaining that our survey was for online users who would generally be unable to visit the bookstore, and our request was approved. We had an 18-percent response rate from students (of 1,295 students surveyed), and a 26-percent response rate from instructors (of 129 instructors surveyed).

We used Google Sheets and Google Docs to compile the responses and develop a report to share with both library administration and the larger university community. The 30-page final report covered detailed breakdowns of responses to each question, including selected free text responses; breakdowns of results by college/department; and an appendix with references, programs surveyed, the call for participation e-mails, and a link to the full dataset. We also prepared an executive summary, where we identified the six most important takeaways from the survey results, and proposed one or two action items for each. For example, one takeaway included in the executive summary was, "Students reported their biggest challenge and frustration was accessing full text." Our proposed action item to address this problem was to work with library technology staff to provide point-of-need help for users unable to access full text articles (e.g., pop-up chat window, instructions within the discovery tool, or video tutorials). We submitted the report to our interim library director, who reviewed it and then shared it with the rest of the library staff and our campus's associate vice chancellor of Curricular Affairs & Student Academic Achievement, who has responsibilities in the assessment of student learning activities and institutional accountability.

Completing the needs assessment has given us a solid evidence base to help us make informed decisions about how to improve and expand our online learning library services. We have already made progress on some of our action items, including identifying new ways to promote our embedded services, developing new point-of-need help tools, and finding better ways to communicate with our users. Our efforts have also helped inspire a future larger-scale assessment of our information literacy instruction program.

Bottom Line: We created a 10-item e-mailed survey using Google Forms to assess the library use and support needs of online students and instructors at our institution. The results of the survey have helped us make informed decisions about how to improve and expand our online learning library services, including promotion, new tools, and better communication. The full needs assessment report can be viewed here: http://bit.ly/2D8K7AI.

Get to Know Your Instructors

Faculty and instructors are among your most important allies in promoting library services to online and distance learning students. However, they are not always aware of what is available to them and their students. Fortunately, there are a number of studies on instructor awareness and use of library resources that can be helpful. Many include suggested questions or themes to find out about your stakeholders.

Questions to consider:

- What do instructors know about library services to distance/online learners?
- What do instructors need or want from you/the library?
- What do instructors expect students to know about the library?
- Who are the potential partners who might be willing to work with you?

Case Study: Assessing Faculty Use of Library Services and Resources in the Learning Management System

Emily Deal, MSIS, Distance Learning Librarian,
University of Louisiana at Lafayette

The University of Louisiana at Lafayette is the second-largest public university in Louisiana, with an enrollment of approximately 19,000 students. In the fall of 2016, nearly 6 percent were enrolled in a program taught entirely online, and an additional 24 percent of students took at least one online or hybrid class. The content of online classes is delivered via the learning management system (LMS) Moodle, and a Moodle course shell is created for every class section each semester, including those that are taught face to face. Instructors who teach face-to-face classes are not required to use Moodle, but many do so to enhance and supplement the content delivered in their classes. Starting in 2012, I began offering a suite of services and resources to help faculty integrate the library into Moodle, including video tutorials, subject guides, and embedded librarian services. The services were initially created to help distance learning faculty, but they are now available to all teaching faculty at the university.

In spring 2017, I created an online survey using SurveyMonkey that was designed to examine how all faculty integrate library services and resources into the LMS. The survey also asked faculty who do not integrate the library into Moodle to explain why not. To reach as many faculty as possible, a link to the eight-question survey was distributed via

the university's faculty e-mail listserv (to view the survey, see https://goo
.gl/forms/0OoINRKOLPBJSoOB2). Eighty-three faculty members completed the survey (around 11 percent of total faculty). Of the respondents, half indicated that they only teach face-to-face classes, while the
other half responded that they frequently, sometimes, or rarely teach
online or hybrid classes. Approximately half of all respondents indicated
that they frequently or sometimes integrate library services and resources
into Moodle.

Responses were analyzed and coded thematically. One major theme
that emerged from the survey responses was the need to better publicize
the library services offered and to educate faculty on how to use them.
Of the faculty who answered that they rarely or never integrate library
services and resources into Moodle, nearly 30 percent indicated that the
reason was that they are not familiar with what the library offers. Another
47 percent indicated that they do not know how to incorporate library
services and resources into Moodle. One respondent wrote, "I honestly
didn't know that these resources were able to be used in Moodle; I plan to
make them available now that I know!" Others wrote that they would like
more short informational sessions or workshops on how to effectively integrate the library into Moodle, and one respondent requested a web page
with instructions on how to include the library in Moodle. An online
guide for faculty already exists, but clearly needs to be promoted more
widely so that faculty are aware of it.

Another emergent theme was the need to improve faculty understanding of copyright issues when integrating class readings into the LMS.
When asked how they provide access to library resources in Moodle,
nearly 78 percent of respondents indicated that they upload PDFs directly
into Moodle, which may violate copyright laws or licensing agreements
with the library's electronic resource vendors. Less than 4 percent indicated that they use EBSCO Curriculum Builder, a plug-in tool that allows
instructors to easily create lists with links to readings in the LMS in accor-
dance with copyright laws and vendor licensing agreements for electronic
resources. Promoting the Curriculum Builder tool and encouraging faculty
to direct students to readings via the use of persistent links, rather than
uploaded PDFs, may help eliminate potential violations of copyright or
licensing agreements.

Finally, many faculty also suggested that the library could better support students by continuing to grow the collections and resources available. Nearly 10 percent of faculty who responded to the survey stated that
the reason they do not incorporate library services and resources into
Moodle is because the library does not provide access to services or
resources that their students need. When asked what additional resources

they would like to see made available, several faculty requested specific journals and databases for their classes, providing an opportunity for the library to strengthen its collection development practices. Other faculty requested more video tutorials for students on how to use the library. Though we have several tutorials already available, faculty requests for additional videos serve as a reminder that the library should both continue to develop new tutorials and better promote the ones already created.

We determined that a multipronged effort to improve the promotion of and education about library services and resources will be the best way to reach as many faculty as possible. We plan to post more frequently to the university's faculty listserv to inform faculty about existing services and resources, and liaison librarians will work with faculty in their departments to provide workshops that will improve awareness of services offered. We are also discussing creating a regular library newsletter to keep faculty informed and abreast of library services and resources. We may repeat the survey to see if improved promotion and education about library services and resources have increased their use in the LMS.

Bottom Line: Publicizing library services and resources and educating faculty about their use are keys to ensuring the successful, copyright-compliant integration of library services and resources into the LMS.

Marketing

The information you have gathered will inform the marketing of library services. Find out where and how library services are marketed to instructors and students. Find out what the process is for developing marketing and promotional materials and who needs to approve what. You don't want to send something out to the online population only to find out it should have been vetted at a higher level. See Chapter 8 for more on marketing to online populations.

The Curriculum

Online education programs vary greatly from institution to institution. Some colleges and universities have a limited number of online programs, such as nursing or business or programs focused on graduate education. Others have a broad scope of online courses in all disciplines and at all levels. Take some time to understand which courses and degrees the institution offers online, where these programs are housed, and who is the best contact for each of these programs.

Program Goals

Most colleges and departments will have some kind of curriculum plan. Familiarize yourself with these for each department that offers online learning. If you can get copies of course syllabi, it can be very helpful to see what sources the instructors are recommending. It can also help you identify where information literacy skills are addressed in the curriculum; those courses make good targets for an embedded librarian. See Chapter 6 for more on embedded librarianship.

Some disciplines and schools have professional standards that they want students to meet upon graduation. If that is the case, do some research to find out what information literacy skills the students need to demonstrate.

Information Literacy Instruction

Will you be taking over a LIB 101 online course? Are you expected to create one? How is instruction for online students currently handled? This can be quite a daunting topic but probably represents a significant portion of your job description. Find out about the synchronous and asynchronous instruction at your library. This includes tutorials, credit and noncredit courses, one-on-one consultations, and "one-shots."

Questions to consider:

- What is the current course load for a librarian at your institution?
- What instruction, if any, did your predecessor do?
- Who creates asynchronous materials? Is there technical support to create videos, tutorials, and other materials?
- How and when are materials updated? Whose responsibility is it?
- How often are the asynchronous materials used? By whom?
- Are any of these materials assigned to a class or group of students?

If you are not familiar with online instruction pedagogy, this would be a good time to do some reading! Chapter 5 has more on this topic.

Collections and Resources

Access to library resources is one of the "principles of entitlement" emphasized in the *Standards*, and many libraries have put policies in place to serve online and distance learners, even if they do not have a librarian who is designated to serve this population. Distance learning students tend to focus on what is available online and immediately available (Joo & Choi, 2016). If an item is not immediately available, they move on to the next item. In addition, online learners often do not think of the library as the place to go for finding research literature. They may also be unfamiliar with services like interlibrary loan or having the library mail books to them (Huwiler, 2015).

It is not always easy to figure out what resources distance and online students are using. Although many vendors will track downloads, they do not necessarily track where the user is located. Check with the staff managing the library's e-resources to see what user data you might be able to access.

Questions to consider:

- What resources are available online, and which are not?
- Do the resources you have online match the curriculum?
- What are the policies in terms of purchasing eBooks, textbooks, or other online resources?
- Is there any way to find out what online students are using? Who can access usage stats?
- How do online learners use library resources?
- How do your online learners find out about what resources are available to them?
- What funding sources are available? How are these being used?

One question that will very likely come up is copyright and fair use of library materials in the online classroom. Instructors may not always know how they can use materials online and may seek help from you. Does your institution have a copyright officer or someone else who has expertise in this area? If not, are you expected to provide guidance? The ALA provides a copyright guide for librarians: https://libguides.ala.org/copyright/general.

Tools and Technology

Technology and online learning go together, so a good understanding of the technological challenges that your learners face is very important. Determine the technologies students need to successfully access library and other university resources and the technologies you will need to assist them.

- What tools do you need to successfully replicate the user experience? When you are helping a student troubleshoot, it can be very useful if you can see what they see. Remote desktop access allows you to see a student's computer.
- LMS (Canvas, Blackboard, Moodle, etc.)—Ideally, your institution will have one LMS that everyone uses. However, in some institutions, every department or college has its own, which adds a layer of complexity to the situation.
- Webinar/videoconferencing software—What is available to you? If the institution or library does not have a subscription, what free tools can you use?

- LibGuides or other content management system—Do you have access to the library website? Can you update your pages? Are there standards or guidelines you need to meet?
- Do you have access to a webcam, microphone, and laptop?
- Does your institution have a site license to a survey platform?
- Are there media services on your campus that can help you?
- Is there a service to help ensure the resources you create comply with the Americans with Disabilities Act (U.S. Department of Justice, n.d.)?
- In addition, you may need access to technology or software to do your job, such as software for tutorial creation, screen-capturing software, and video or audio captioning services. You may want to wait until you have a better idea of what you want to create or produce before purchasing new technology.

One significant concern for online learners is seamless access to online resources. Those of us who are located on a large or main campus will often have very good Internet access, but that will not be the case for all your students. As an online education librarian, you may find that students expect you to provide technical support as well as research support. If a student cannot access resources or download articles, they will not use the library. For more information about online access to library services and resources, see Chapter 9.

Questions to consider:

- How are off-campus users authenticated? In most cases, the library will use some kind of service to provide off-campus access to online resources. How does this work? Can you create an interface for staff use that mirrors what your students experience?
- Is there online tech support for distance education students? Unfortunately, online learners are often on their own when it comes to technology, and they often don't know if the issue they are having is a library problem (the services are not working correctly) or a computer problem (e.g., Java is not properly configured on their machine). You will need to help them untangle the issue and send them to the right place once you do know where the problem lies.
- What technology requirements (if any) does the university have for online or distance learners?

One additional suggestion is to consider taking an online course, if you have not done so already. There are many free options available. Being an online learner yourself will give you a better understanding of the online learner's perspective and give you some "street-cred" with your students. See the online world from their point of view.

Conclusion

This chapter posed many questions for you to consider. Depending on the type and size of your institution, not all of them will be applicable. Document your processes and procedures. Keep track of your ideas and suggestions. And, as always, reach out to your fellow distance and online learning librarians. We welcome your questions and contributions.

CHAPTER TWO

Learn about Your Patrons and Set Goals to Serve Them

Joelle E. Pitts

Introduction

Setting strategic and achievable goals is an important step in any professional library endeavor. Much has been written about the importance of goal setting and how to set smart goals. This chapter offers only a cursory treatment of the literature and best practices of goal setting in general, but is a foundational element of this volume and in serving online patrons in general. This is because the scope of serving library patrons in an increasingly digital world is very broad. It is easy to become lost in the magnitude of opportunities, best practices, tips, traps, and other considerations for serving online patrons, especially if you or your library has not fully ventured into this arena before now. It is critically important that you combine the information and data you gather with the mission of your organization to formulate realistic, measurable, user-centered goals. Your library can't be all things to all people, but you can develop great services and resources to meet user needs. The following sections will cover the basics of how to conduct a needs analysis of your online population, make evidence-based decisions from your results, and create short- and long-term goals.

Learn about Your Patrons

User-Centeredness

After taking stock of your library (see Chapter 1), you might be pleasantly surprised by the number of services and resources already available to your online patrons. You might even find that your library has already addressed the most critical gaps in access, instruction, or virtual reference. If so, your goal-setting efforts might focus on making weaker services more robust or marketing to new audiences. More likely, your analysis revealed several areas for growth and development or highlighted populations you are not currently, but should be, serving. In any case, don't immediately dive into the work of filling gaps before you know which ones are most critical to your particular patron base. For instance, your library might not currently offer a video reference service, but that doesn't mean your patrons necessarily want that option. The decisions you make and the goals you set need to be based not only on what your library can and can't offer, but on what your patrons need the most. Adopt a user-centered approach to setting goals in order to create services and resources your online patrons need.

At the most basic, being user-centered means becoming familiar with your users and their needs and making decisions according to those needs. There are many user-centered frameworks. One of the more robust is the user-centered design (UCD) approach. The U.S. Department of Health and Human Services offers one process for using UCD that we've found to be simple and easily adaptable. It defines the design process as being "based upon an explicit understanding of users, tasks, and environments; . . . driven and refined by user-centered evaluation; and [which] addresses the whole user experience" (U.S. Department of Health and Human Services, n.d., para. 2).

The phases in the UCD approach are described as follows:

- **Specify the context of use:** Identify the people who will use the product, what they will use it for, and under what conditions they will use it.
- **Specify requirements:** Identify any business requirements or user goals that must be met for the product to be successful.
- **Create design solutions:** This part of the process may be done in stages, building from a rough concept to a complete design.
- **Evaluate designs:** Evaluation—ideally through usability testing with actual users—is as integral as quality testing is to good software development.

Figure 2.1 illustrates this process.

Many libraries have already dabbled in the UCD realm. Patron-driven acquisition, purchase-on-demand, usability testing, and other practices are widely used not only to build better patron experiences but also in an attempt to match ever-shrinking budgets with the most critical patron needs. Regardless of the specific practice, the first step in any user-centered approach to development is a needs analysis.

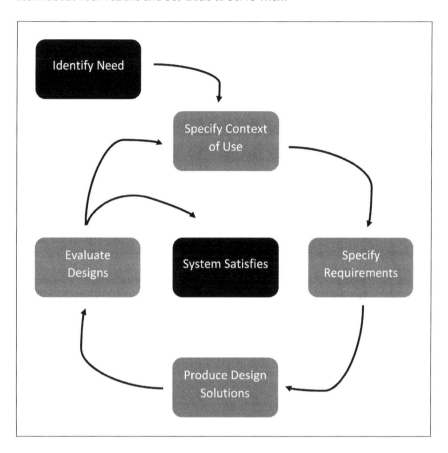

Figure 2.1 Image from: https://www.usability.gov/what-and-why/user-centered-design.html.

Needs Analysis

There are many forms and strategies for conducting needs analysis. Fields as diverse as instructional design and human resources management have developed and refined methods for this activity. Depending on your area of practice, you may find it helpful to identify a needs analysis framework that best aligns with your role and philosophy. For instance, if you are a public services librarian, an instructional design needs analysis might seem most relevant to you. If you are a systems librarian, a software needs analysis might be a better model.

Needs analyses for online populations are often difficult to conduct and interpret. Even the broader design literature is scarce in terms of best practices for needs analyses of those you might never see in person or interact with synchronously. One approach to consider is the Blended Librarians Adapted ADDIE Model (BLAAM) approach, proposed by Steven Bell and John Shank in their book, *Academic Librarianship by Design* (2007). The BLAAM model instructs librarians to use a practical and resource-optimizing approach to the ADDIE instructional design framework, including a truncated needs assessment. See Chapter 5 for more about instructional design and the ADDIE model. They suggest that instruction librarians take some time to assess the learning situation in order to better understand what the faculty member's learning outcomes are and where their students are deficient in achieving them. This approach can be utilized in almost every scenario involving online patrons, for example:

- Are online patrons experiencing access problems that keep them from the materials they need?
- What do online patrons know about our services, and what don't they know?
- Can online patrons successfully download articles or other electronic materials the majority of the time?
- Are online patrons utilizing virtual reference services? If not, why not?

It may also be helpful to assess the needs of potential patrons: those who could access the library online and choose not to, or those who don't even know they can use the library at all. The latter group will be much harder to identify, but use of surveys, marketing campaigns, and social media outreach strategies might ferret out enough of these potential users that you can draw conclusions about strategies to reach them in greater numbers. Typical information gathered in a needs analysis includes demographics, preferences in terms of service and resource use, access to the Internet, digital literacy, and the time of day online patrons want/need help. These are examples of questions a library might pose to an online patron during a needs analysis:

- Are you able to come to the physical library building for help or resources?
- What kind of Internet service do you have at home (e.g., dial-up, cable, wireless, satellite, cellular)?
- What time of day are you most likely to use the library?
- On a scale of one to five, how comfortable are you using a chat or videoconferencing service to request help from the library?
- Do you know where to find databases, books, help options, and so on?
- What barriers prevent you from using the library?
- Do you require assistive technology to access online materials?

Table 2.1 provides a checklist that is not exhaustive but includes examples of information about your online patrons that may be relevant during a needs analysis.

Table 2.1 Questions for needs analysis.

General information/ demographics	Access to and comfort level with digital technology	Awareness and usage of the library
Age and number of children in the home, languages spoken, education levels	Type of Internet connection	Knowledge that they can use the library online
Household income	Type of connected device, use of assistive technology	Awareness of specific online services and resources
Location	Comfort or self-efficacy levels with digital technologies used by library	Preferences for or gaps in online services and resources
Major or area of research or information needs	Technical barriers to using the library online	Time of day library is accessed online

There are many different tactics for conducting this kind of primary research on your online population. Your library may already do this at some level; for instance, many academic libraries utilize the LibQUAL+ survey which "helps libraries solicit, track, understand, and act upon users' opinions of service quality" (Association of Research Libraries, n.d.). Find as much existing patron data as you can before you start reaching out to patrons, such as web usage statistics, previous user data, enrollment reports, census data, and market research reports. Once you have exhausted the existing resources, determine the best approach for your population. Techniques for learning about online users include:

- Awareness surveys (via e-mail or direct mail)
- Virtual focus groups
- Instant feedback forms embedded into online platforms
- "Pre" surveys for online courses
- Individual conversations via phone calls or online interviews

As with most market research, your efforts will be more successful if you incentivize this activity for your population by offering some kind of compensation in exchange for their responses such as gift cards, flash drives, or food. You could also consider offering one big prize like a tablet or other device that all of the surveyed population would be eligible for in a drawing. Check with your accounting office to learn more about local legal restrictions for prizes.

You can also engage in secondary market research to learn more about your community and your potential patrons. Free tools such as the Claritas PRIZM Premier Segmentation System (https://claritas360.claritas.com/my bestsegments/) allow you to look up demographic and lifestyle information by zip code. Click on a few of the PRIZM market segment types and read what they have to say. Even if the segment descriptions seem far-fetched, you will be able to gather basic demographic information, including household income and composition, age, and race and ethnicity information. Government agencies such as the U.S. Census Bureau (https://census.gov/) and Statistics Canada (https://www.statcan.gc.ca/eng/start) can also provide population numbers and other data. Local government and your community chamber of commerce might also have public data you can mine. If you are in an academic setting, check with your online learning department, registrar, or university or library planning office to see what data you can find about your potential population.

Evidence-Based Decision Making

All of the research you have completed on your library and your online patrons will inform the next steps you take toward serving them. Pair this kind of research with a review of the library literature on serving online patrons, and you will have a solid base of evidence to use when you set goals. This is the process of evidence-based decision making at its most basic. It allows you to move forward with goals, projects, and directives with greater confidence.

Called evidenced-based practice in the medical world, doctors, nurses, and other health professionals use a three-dimensional framework to make public health decisions. The framework includes contextual evidence, experiential evidence, and the best available research evidence. In the same way, you can combine the insights you gained from taking stock of your library (experiential evidence) and the primary and secondary market research you completed (contextual evidence) with takeaways from the library literature on serving online patrons (research evidence) to create sound short-term and long-term goals.

This process allows you to avoid or at least mitigate the "if we build it, will they come?" question that many libraries struggle with when implementing new projects. You can also use your research and data to propose and justify new expenditures to your board or administration. If you decide to build it, it will be because all the data points to it as the best way to serve online patrons.

Setting Goals to Serve Online Patrons

Setting goals based on your research is essential because they provide you with a road map for better service to online patrons. They enable you to act on your interpretations of the data while minimizing lower-priority activities. Well-crafted goals can help you avoid burnout and maintain a sense of progress in the face of what can often be an overwhelming number of choices.

There is a mountain of research and literature available on the topic of goal setting. This section will barely skim the surface so as to focus directly on the aspects of goal setting that pertain to online patrons and service environments. There are also many strategies and models for goal-setting that might work better for your library and role therein, but we will focus on the SMART model (Specific, Measurable, Assignable, Realistic, Timely) as an accessible entryway into this practice.

SMART Goals

SMART goals were originally offered by George T. Doran in a 1981 issue of *Management Review* as a method for business managers to operationalize production goals. Since then the acronym has been reused and reimagined in various contexts and environments, including libraries.

As Figure 2.2 illustrates, each letter of the acronym denotes a specific characteristic of a SMART or effective goal:

Specific: Target a specific area for improvement.
Measurable: Quantify or at least suggest an indicator or progress.
Assignable: Specify who will do it.
Realistic: State what results can realistically be achieved, given available resources.
Timely: Specify when the results can be achieved.

When applied to goals created to serve online patrons, consider your time both in terms of hours in the day and in terms of how long it might take you

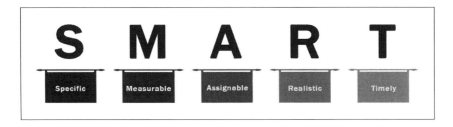

Figure 2.2   SMART goal descriptors.

or your team to learn a new technology, conduct usability testing, or otherwise gain a digital skill necessary for serving this population. You will also want to consider how your goals might be affected by the technology you and your library are using, as well as the technology being utilized most often by your patrons. For example, using a certain software might allow you to better track online usage of a resource, making the goal more measurable. Tailoring a service to suit the needs of mobile phone users might be a specific and measurable goal, but unless your library has staff who understand responsive web design or mobile apps, it might not be assignable, realistic, or timely.

An example of a SMART goal derived from a library needs assessment of online patrons might be *Jane Doe Librarian will lead user services and IT department staff in the purchase and implementation of the Browzine discovery service overlay by three months from today.*

Technical Considerations

Whether considering the actual service or resource being offered online, or the means necessary to market these resources (see Chapter 8), almost all of your goals for online patrons will be mediated by technology in one way or another. Technical projects, including those that involve revamping an online resource or designing and building one from scratch, have a tendency to take longer than estimated. Carefully research the technical parameters of any goal. Consider software/hardware, maintenance, usability, design and development, and expertise required to meet your goals. Ask yourself the following questions during the goal-setting process to ensure you have accounted for most, if not all, potential pitfalls. Though not exhaustive, these questions can help you start thinking about the technical considerations of any project or goal geared toward online patrons:

- Do I or does someone at my library have the skills to build/redesign this project, or can we partner or contract with someone who does? Can their job duties be arranged to accommodate the project?
- What kind of maintenance will this service or resource require once it's built? Who will carry it out?
- Who will be available to troubleshoot for me or for the online patrons if something goes wrong?
- What software will be needed to achieve this goal? Do we have someone who knows how to use it or can learn? How much does it cost?
- Will our online patrons be able to successfully use the resource as it is designed?
- Who will be the contact for any technical vendors or providers? Who will be negotiating the contracts?

The capacity to enact your technical goals may not exist in your library; but don't limit yourself if you are able to look to vendors or other partnerships to complete projects.

Short-Term versus Long-Term Goals for Online Patrons

As with any goal-setting activity, you will want to consider what is achievable in the short term and what is reasonable in the long term. This process is complicated in an online environment due to the rapidly changing nature of the web. According to a 2017 IBM Marketing Cloud Study, 90 percent of the data on the Internet has been created since 2016 and every day we create 2.5 *quintillion* bytes of data. The number of users, amount of information, online platforms, and technologies created to interact with these bytes will only increase as time goes by. That can be a daunting challenge for librarians charged to serve people in this environment, which is why SMART goals are so important to scope the project and define objectives. It also means that you must consider long-term goals carefully. Content and technologies can quickly become obsolete.

A library that spent time and lots of money replacing its VHS tapes with DVDs after 2010 could have instead considered that streaming video would completely revolutionize the way that people consume film media. It could have invested in a product that allows for online streaming and watched media usage go up and access for online patrons improve dramatically. When setting long-term goals, you must carefully study the Internet environment, read technology blogs, follow industry leaders on social media, and otherwise stay connected to the most current conversations. It can be tricky to balance ever-shrinking budgets and organizational priorities with trend and technology analysis on the web. Successful online librarians are able to gauge which trends might best serve their patrons and which have a longer shelf life than others. They are ready to incorporate them into goal-setting activities at the right time.

You can use tools like PEW Research Center studies and Horizon Reports to help make these kinds of long-term decisions. PEW specializes in Internet and technology research. On https://www.pewinternet.org/ you can find a variety of studies and reports on aspects of Internet and technology usage, such as a 2017 report on technology adoption among older adults that concludes that smartphone adoption among seniors nearly quadrupled in the preceding five years (Anderson & Perrin, 2017). Horizon Reports are created annually by EDUCAUSE and provide insights into short-term, mid-term, and longer-term trends, challenges, and technology developments in libraries, museums, and other educational areas. Regular study of technology trends can help improve your ability to make wise choices about where to invest time and resources.

Case Study: The One UWI Library

Arlene Alleyne-Regis, MLIS, Academic Liaison Librarian
Adele Merritt Bernard, MLS, Academic Liaison Librarian
The University of the West Indies

This case study highlights the process used by the University of the West Indies Libraries (the UWI Libraries) to set goals and determine strategy for implementing the Strategic Plan 2017–2022 of the University of the West Indies (The UWI). It summarizes a three-day workshop, where library staff collaborated through discussion, music, and art to identify issues, challenges, and opportunities to chart the path forward for the next five years.

Established in 1948, the UWI was the first higher education provider in the English-speaking Caribbean region. In 2008, the Open Campus was added to the three existing landed campuses on the islands of Barbados, Jamaica, and Trinidad and Tobago, to expand the reach of the university. Using the online education model the UWI now serves students in 17 individual territories, spanning an area of some 1.6 million square miles.

Central to the UWI's Triple A Strategy Framework 2017–2022 (University of the West Indies. (n.d.).) are the strategic goals of Access, Alignment and Agility, and the mandate to operate as the "One UWI" despite the distributed nature and decentralized management of the four campuses. The campus libraries were able to identify unique priority action items, allied to the strategic objectives of Access (improve the quality of teaching, learning and student development), Alignment (increase and improve academic/industry research partnerships), and Agility (foster the digital transformation of the UWI).

The workshop launched with a welcoming activity that used song writing and performances to set the tone for collaboration and creativity. At the end of the first session participants determined the workshop's deliverables. For the purposes of this case study we will focus on the outcome: to identify potential projects for the university's libraries that would advance the strategic objectives of virtualization, teaching and learning, and research and publication.

Participants worked in groups through an iterative process of discussion and voting to determine the judging criteria and to whittle down over 60 project ideas to seven viable projects, prioritizing them based on organizational needs. Criteria such as greatest impact and reach, ease of replication across campuses, mode of service delivery, and achievability within a two- to three-year time frame were applied to select medium- to long-term goals for each project. The groups then worked to develop draft action plans, identify the possible scope of projects, determine the lead on projects and their responsibilities, and list possible resources required.

Of the campus libraries, the Open Campus Libraries and Information Services team was charged with realizing the strategic initiative of the creation of a virtual learning space. The corresponding strategic objective invited librarians to collaborate in the learning process to ensure that the students' time spent online is more focused on problem solving and critical thinking skills. The team met to document its intended work using the accompanying administrative tool—an Initiative Planner disseminated by the university's leadership team.

The planner is designed to assist with determining the targets, major activities, tasks, timelines, personnel, resources, and cost of each activity as well as potential risks and mitigating factors.

Elements of the Initiative Planner with some examples related to our task are given next:

Initiative Title: Creation of a Virtual Learning Space.

Purpose: To advance teaching and learning by encouraging students, staff, and librarians to collaborate in the learning process to ensure that the students time spent online is more focused on problem solving and critical thinking skills.

Target: Library website with interactive self-paced instructional tools on a variety of topics.

Key Performance Indicator: Internal Stakeholders Satisfaction score.

Deliverable(s): Develop eight interactive LibGuides.

Milestone(s): Four interactive LibGuides developed within six months.

Team Members: Interdisciplinary team including librarian, IT personnel, production assistants, graphics and design personnel.

The planner also provides the opportunity to address other aspects, including dates and deadlines, work plan, major activities, tasks, estimated timelines, personnel assignments, resources, costs, and risks and mitigating factors.

Bottom line: Using established procedures for goal-setting can simplify and maximize the efficiency of the process.

Conclusion

Serving online patrons offers a unique set of challenges and requires close attention to online environments and patron needs. After taking stock of what your library currently offers these patrons and before you begin creating new services and resources for them, take time to get to know their unique needs. Conduct a needs assessment and learn more about this population before you reach out to them. UCD and evidence-based decision-making practices can help you set SMART short- and long-term goals that not only make the best use of your time and resources but also best serve your online patrons.

CHAPTER THREE

Inclusive Design

Joelle E. Pitts

Introduction

Online patrons approach libraries from a variety of circumstances. Their location, connection speed, physical and cognitive ability, language proficiency, digital literacy level, socioeconomic status, and many more factors have the potential to affect your ability to provide quality services and resources to this population. Sometimes you will be aware of the circumstances because the patron will disclose that information or there will be some other indicator. More often, you will not know the exact combination of circumstances a particular patron is facing when they make contact with a service point or begin to interact with your online interfaces. When you start taking action on the goals you create (see Chapter 2), it is important to employ a design process that will allow you to serve the most online patrons possible no matter their circumstances.

Inclusivity and equitable services and resources are important aspects of librarianship. It is easier to plan for and create services for people you see and communicate with personally, especially on a regular basis. However, online use of library resources and services is growing, and our professional standards, for example, the Association of College and Research Libraries' Distance Learning Section *Standards for Distance Learning Library Services*, state that it is our duty to provide equitable service. You should not only be aware of your growing online population but should also make a concerted effort to listen to and amplify their voices.

We recommend employing a way of thinking about inclusive environments called universal design (UD). Universal design was born out of the disability rights movements of the mid-20th century and focused primarily on the design of built or physical environments that were inclusive of people with a wide variety of abilities. In recent years, the UD concept has been adopted and adapted into other fields and disciplines, most notably for this volume, in libraries using the Universal Design for Learning (UDL) model. The concept of *environment* has also been expanded to include the digital spaces where we do business, teach, learn, and interact with others.

One basic description of universal design is offered by Steinfeld and Maisel (2012):

> Universal design is a process that enables and empowers a diverse population by improving human performance, health, wellness, and social participation.

This description highlights the need to design environments that enable human beings to function most effectively. It makes life "easier, healthier, and friendlier" (Steinfeld & Maisel 2012). Libraries already embrace these principles. Universal design aligns with the *Standards for Distance Learning Library Services*, and many of the activities and professional development opportunities offered by various sections and committees within the American Library Association incorporate these ideas even if they are not employing the specific vocabulary.

There are many texts, articles, and websites available to help you better understand universal design. Some suggestions are in the Appendix. We do not repeat that information here in detail. This chapter offers a basic look into the universal design process and how it can be adapted to serving online library patrons.

Principles of Universal Design

There are many ways to approach the design and creation of inviting and widely usable environments. The approach you take will depend on a number of factors, including budget, design and development expertise, and time. Table 3.1 illustrates the principles of universal design as first formulated by The Center for Universal Design at North Carolina State University. They are not exhaustive and not library-specific, but serve as a foundation for understanding the elements and intent behind this way of thinking.

Although these and many other universal design principles were written for people with differing physical abilities, you can no doubt begin to see how employing these principles could help a wide range of individuals experience better service and access to library resources. For example, principle 3 dictates simple and intuitive environments. Creating web interfaces and online forms that are easy to use and intuitive not only helps your online patrons who may be struggling with various physical, cognitive, or location-based

Table 3.1 Principles of universal design, Copyright © 1997 NC State University, the Center for Universal Design.

Principles	Guidelines
Principle 1: Equitable Use The design is useful and marketable to people with diverse abilities.	1a. Provide the same means of use for all users: identical whenever possible; equivalent when not. 1b. Avoid segregating or stigmatizing any users. 1c. Provisions for privacy, security, and safety should be equally available to all users. 1d. Make the design appealing to all users.
Principle 2: Flexibility in Use The design accommodates a wide range of individual preferences and abilities.	2a. Provide choice in methods of use. 2b. Accommodate right- or left-handed access and use. 2c. Facilitate the user's accuracy and precision. 2d. Provide adaptability to the user's pace.
Principle 3: Simple and Intuitive Use Use of the design is easy to understand, regardless of the user's experience, knowledge, language skills, or current concentration level.	3a. Eliminate unnecessary complexity. 3b. Be consistent with user expectations and intuition. 3c. Accommodate a wide range of literacy and language skills. 3d. Arrange information consistent with its importance. 3e. Provide effective prompting and feedback during and after task completion.
Principle 4: Perceptible Information The design communicates necessary information effectively to the user, regardless of ambient conditions or the user's sensory abilities.	4a. Use different modes (pictorial, verbal, tactile) for redundant presentation of essential information. 4b. Provide adequate contrast between essential information and its surroundings. 4c. Maximize "legibility" of essential information. 4d. Differentiate elements in ways that can be described (i.e., make it easy to give instructions or directions). 4e. Provide compatibility with a variety of techniques or devices used by people with sensory limitations.

(Continued)

Table 3.1 (Continued)

Principles	Guidelines
Principle 5: Tolerance for Error The design minimizes hazards and the adverse consequences of accidental or unintended actions.	5a. Arrange elements to minimize hazards and errors: most used elements, most accessible; hazardous elements eliminated, isolated, or shielded. 5b. Provide warnings of hazards and errors. 5c. Provide fail-safe features. 5d. Discourage unconscious action in tasks that require vigilance.
Principle 6: Low Physical Effort The design can be used efficiently and comfortably and with a minimum of fatigue.	6a. Allow user to maintain a neutral body position. 6b. Use reasonable operating forces. 6c. Minimize repetitive actions. 6d. Minimize sustained physical effort.
Principle 7: Size and Space for Approach and Use Appropriate size and space is provided for approach, reach, manipulation, and use regardless of user's body size, posture, or mobility.	7a. Provide a clear line of sight to important elements for any seated or standing user. 7b. Make reach to all components comfortable for any seated or standing user. 7c. Accommodate variations in hand and grip size. 7d. Provide adequate space for the use of assistive devices or personal assistance.

barriers, but it also helps all patrons who might find themselves in front of these interfaces at some point in time. Universal design allows us to focus on making the user experience better for everyone in the process of helping those who need accommodations.

Universal Design for Online Library Patrons

You can apply the seven principles of universal design to library services and interfaces online patrons might encounter. There are many lenses through which you could approach this application, but to keep it simple, this chapter focuses on considerations for mediated and unmediated environments.

In the simplest terms, mediated environments are those that require a human on the other end. For online library patrons, mediated encounters with library staff typically happen through service points such as reference or interlibrary loan. Despite the advent of self-service technologies and options, most libraries still make use of actively staffed service points. Help desks and live online classes or seminars are the obvious examples, but there are other ways you can interact with online patrons synchronously, including scheduled consultations and regular engagement or "office hours" within a course delivered through a learning management system (LMS). These mediated encounters are typically conducted through some type of technology, at the very least through a phone or e-mail conversation.

Unmediated or asynchronous library encounters are those that occur without a library employee actively present and monitoring the interaction. Every time a patron interacts with online databases, catalogs, webforms, LibGuides, and so on, they are having an unmediated encounter with a library.

It is important to apply universal design considerations to both types of encounters online patrons might face.

Equitable Use: Libraries should ensure that in-person and online patrons are provided equitable services and resources. Service hours, help options, and instructional opportunities are examples of mediated activities that must be designed equitably. For instance, if in-person patrons can get help from a librarian until 10:00 PM, provide live help services to online patrons during that time frame as well. Unmediated encounters should also be made equitable, and you can take steps to ensure that your technology is not creating unnecessary barriers that in-person patrons don't have to overcome. For instance, you don't ask in-person patrons to self-identify what their status or educational level is before you answer their questions at the reference desk, so you shouldn't do it through filtering or other identifying inputs in the online environment either.

Flexible Use: It can be difficult to find balance between functionality and simplicity in online environments. On one hand, we want to provide as many options for access and service as possible. On the other, we know we should design our online spaces to be simple and elegant. One way to strike this balance with mediated interactions is to develop and train staff to work with a variety of technologies and options. E-mail and phone conversations don't require too much development or training time. But services like virtual chat, embedded interactions within LMS systems, and web conferencing can require more. It is also important to develop a set of quality and customer service standards for online-mediated interactions just as you would for in-person interactions. Online patrons and those who use both in-person and online services will come to expect a high level of service quality in whatever format you offer. Ensuring that quality across the range of options will provide them with a greater level of flexibility. Unmediated environments also need to be flexible. Options for obtaining help or training should be obvious and easy to use. Creating transcribed videos or other tutorials that demonstrate the use of unmediated environments is helpful, as are research guides and other static learning materials. It is also important for online environments to be flexible in terms of device and platform. Ensure interfaces are responsive to multiple devices (including mobile platforms) and function as expected across all major browsers.

Simple and Intuitive Use: In both mediated and unmediated environments library services and resources should be simple and intuitive to use. They should be discoverable without much clicking, and the functionality should be easy to master once found. Online patrons should not have to alter their questions or approach interactions with library staff any differently than they would in person, with the exception of the interaction being facilitated through some sort of web or other technologies. Unmediated environments should be as simple as possible, should be clearly labeled, and should avoid library jargon. For example, don't refer to a web-scale discovery tool. Rather, tell your patrons what they will find if they use the tool: books and articles. It's also critical to employ best practices when writing for online environments. White space, short bulleted lists, and text written at an eighth grade reading level are examples of such standards. The Nielsen Norman Group is an organization that offers widely used training and guidelines on writing for the web. Others can be found in the Appendix. Online patrons don't often care what technology is driving the interfaces and functions they are using—they just want the technology to work without spending a lot of time and effort learning how to use it.

Perceptible Information: This principle applies primarily to unmediated environments, though there are a few situations where using multiple sensory formats can be useful during synchronous online instructional activities, such as using both microphone and chat features of a web conferencing software during a live session. There are many different ways people learn and transfer information, so it can be helpful to provide information in multiple formats. A good example is using screenshots of library interfaces along with text instructions when designing tutorials to accommodate those with a preference for images as well as those with a preference for text. Video captions and time-stamped transcripts not only have the potential to help individuals with low hearing, but they are also often utilized by English language learners, individuals with cognitive or other learning impairments, and those who require multiple readings or attempts to accomplish tasks. Taking these measures also helps ensure the accessibility of information for those using assistive technology (e.g., screen readers) to engage with your online content.

Tolerance for Error: Online environments can be riddled with the potential for error. Almost everyone has experienced computers crashing, blue "screens of death," service interruptions, and other errors. These errors can be very frustrating for any patron, but potentially more so for online patrons who have no means to try again on a different device at a physical library location. There are several ways to mitigate or at least plan for errors during mediated interactions with online patrons:

- Test the software you plan to use for teaching or reference sessions before using it live, and log in a few minutes ahead of the scheduled start time to run updates, test audio, and speakers. If possible, test briefly with the patron ahead of time.
- Offer alternative means of communication within the platform you are using to communicate; for example, allow participants to use the chat window in case their microphone does not work.
- Keep troubleshooting web pages or resources handy during the session so that you can readily help those having difficulty. Have a list of go-to troubleshooting tips at hand to diagnose and solve common issues such as browser incompatibility.
- Offer to follow up with the patron when technical errors occur.

It is even more important that unmediated environments remain as error-free as possible since the patron will not have immediate access to a library staff member to help troubleshoot or arrive at the needed information. Working with skilled web designers and programmers can help reduce the numbers of errors patrons encounter online, as can several rounds of in-house user testing before a product or space is rolled out for public use. Assigning an individual or department to monitor these systems for errors is wise, as are standing maintenance procedures for the various systems the library uses. For example, Springshare's LibGuides system creates a broken link report that system administrators can periodically run and use to fix errors. Running periodic accessibility checks through software like AMP (Accessibility Management Platform) or the WAVE tool from webaim.org is also beneficial. Finally, periodic usability testing can be helpful to ferret out the common errors users encounter. Even if you are not able to recruit online patrons to participate in the tests, you can still gain valuable insights that will help you better serve those who navigate your online environments. There are many methods to conduct usability testing. The method you choose will depend on the time you have available for the task, your budget, and the technology you have available and are comfortable using. A simple way to start is task testing: measuring whether a patron can complete an assigned task on your website. Basic recording software such as Screencast-O-Matic can help you document what paths patrons are using to explore your site if you plan to conduct in-person tests. See the Appendix for more tools and resources on usability testing.

   Low Physical Effort; Size and Space for Approach and Use: Principles 6 and 7 apply primarily to physical library spaces but should be considered when designing services and resources for online patrons. What must a patron physically do in order to make use of the resource or service? Will they have to speak using a microphone? Return a book to a physical mailing center after use? Constantly use their fingers to enhance the size of text or other content on a mobile device? It can be easy to imagine that online patrons using the library have no physical barriers, but your design process should cover as many scenarios as possible in both mediated and unmediated circumstances.

Standards and Checklists

Once you determine your organizational standards and guidelines, create a policy around them. Codifying standards is one important way you can ensure they are understood and implemented by everyone in your organization. Provide those who work with online environments with a checklist they can easily use to ensure compliance. An example checklist is offered in Figure 3.1, based on well-known writing for the web, accessibility, and usability standards.

Accessibility
- ☐ Images have ALT text.
- ☐ Links and files should open in the same window. Exceptions are labeled properly.
- ☐ Links to non-HTML files include the file type.
- ☐ No flash or inaccessible forms of content are present.
- ☐ Color has not been used as the sole means of conveying meaning.
- ☐ PDFs and other files are rendered in a format accessible for screen readers.

Research Guide Structure
- ☐ The landing page tells users what they will find in my guide.
- ☐ Tabs for common sections match the list of recommended tab titles.
- ☐ Headings and subheadings are used to help organize content and make it scannable.
- ☐ The most important content on each page is presented at the top.

Text Structure
- ☐ Content is tailored for audience and includes context for its use.
- ☐ Tables, videos, or graphics are used to present content in a digestible format.
- ☐ Paragraphs are limited to 3 to 5 short sentences when possible.
- ☐ Lists of resources or links are comprised of five items or fewer.
- ☐ Links and resources are annotated to briefly tell the user what they are and why they are important.

Writing Conventions
- ☐ Names for products, apps, and tools match the official spelling.
- ☐ Acronyms are used sparingly and are spelled out on the first occurrence.
- ☐ Library jargon is used sparingly and given context for new users.
- ☐ The text is typo and error free.

Permissions, Images, and Videos
- ☐ For copyrighted works, permission is obtained from and provides attribution to the creator.
- ☐ Images use as small a file size as possible to reduce download time.
- ☐ Videos are accurately captioned or, if captioning is not possible, have a time-stamped transcript file presented in PDF format.
- ☐ Internally-produced videos are shorter than 5 minutes with a file size less than 20GB and have 640×480 resolution or higher.
- ☐ Internally-produced videos identify the Libraries as the author. Externally-created videos are attributed to their source.

Figure 3.1 Sample standards checklist.

Universal Design for Learning

The U.S. Department of Education's Higher Education Opportunity Act of 2008 provides a definition of UDL and is re-created here:

SEC. 103. Additional Definitions

(24) UNIVERSAL DESIGN FOR LEARNING.
  The term "universal design for learning" means a scientifically valid framework for guiding educational practice that—

(A) Provides flexibility in ways information is presented, in the ways students respond or demonstrate knowledge and skills, and in the ways students are engaged; and
(B) Reduces barriers in instruction, provides appropriate accommodations, supports, and challenges, and maintains high achievement expectations for all students, including students with disabilities and students who are limited English proficient [*sic*]

Retrieved from: https://www2.ed.gov/policy/highered/leg/hea08/index .html.

Like its parent term, universal design, UDL specifically requires that accommodations are made to provide equitable learning opportunities for those with varying abilities and proficiencies. And like its parent term, we can apply UDL broadly in order to design learning environments that not only help patrons with unique challenges overcome barriers but provide a better experience for everyone else as well.

Libraries of all kinds are charged with facilitating learning within their communities. Academic and school libraries have led the way in creating instructional opportunities for patrons in the form of classes, workshops, and information literacy integration within program curricula, but many have a long way to go in providing equitable opportunities to online learners. When teaching online students and patrons, you can rely on the principles of UDL to help you craft meaningful and informative learning experiences.

An easy-to-conceptualize (but far-less-easy-to-implement) approach is to accept that what works for in-person library instruction won't necessarily work for online instructional environments. Clicking through databases and finding books in the stacks might work for a traditional in-person "one-shot" session, but won't work as well for online learners. Obviously, online patrons won't be able to look for books on the physical shelves. It is less obvious that database demonstrations in an online environment, while possible, don't allow for students to follow along on their own device as they would for in-person sessions because they are using their device's screen or monitor to watch what you are doing. It is a passive experience online, whereas the in-person students are allowed to both watch and try it out on their own. UDL advocates for instructors not to simply reformat existing instructional practices for new platforms or assistive technologies, but to redesign the instruction altogether to allow for more flexibility in mastery of the subject area. In the previous case, a librarian might create a short screencast modeling the database search for online students to watch on their own time, while using the mediated or synchronous class time to have a discussion about how to evaluate the materials they might encounter in the database and why some carry more authority than others.

An in-depth treatment of the topic of instruction for online patrons will be provided in Chapter 5.

Case Study: Practical Techniques for Teaching Online in a UDL-Friendly Way

Denyse Rodrigues, MA, MISt, E-Learning and Library Research Services Librarian, *Mount Saint Vincent University*
Amy Lorencz, MLIS, Metadata and Copyright Librarian, *Saint Mary's University*
Terri Milton, MLIS, Campus Librarian, *Nova Scotia Community College*

Mount Saint Vincent University (MSVU) is a small university in Nova Scotia, Canada. Librarians are responsible for teaching LIBR 2100: Introduction to Research in the Information Age, a for-credit, information literacy, humanities elective. The course is delivered three semesters a year in both face-to-face and online formats. Each section is capped at 30 students.

In 2016, we redeveloped the online section of the course with principles from universal design for learning (UDL) in mind. We invited an instructional designer, the learning management system (Moodle) administrator, and the disability services coordinator to meet regularly during the course redevelopment process. We reviewed the course goals and objectives to update them, not only to include the Association of College and Research Libraries information literacy frameworks, but also to incorporate the UDL principles of providing multiple means of engagement, representation, and action. Based on our understanding of the UDL principles we embraced the mantra of options, options, options, as we undertook the work of redesigning and teaching the online course.

Provide Multiple Means of Engagement

In planning the assessment component of the course, we used a term project comprising distinct assignments that built upon one another so that students learned from mistakes and developed their research skills in incremental ways in a supportive environment. Students chose their own research topic, thereby increasing ownership and engagement with their project. The assignment instructions guided the students in making the transition from personal interest to a scholarly approach, fostering a research mind-set. Reflective questions were included to gauge their engagement with their projects and encourage self-awareness in their learning process. All coursework included evaluation guideline rubrics to provide transparency in their learning process. We instituted a resubmission policy for coursework so that students had an opportunity to correct their errors before moving on to the next stage of the research process.

How Did This Work in Practice?

The reflective questions proved useful in measuring engagement, and on occasion, they were instrumental in prompting conversations with students to refine their project selection. The resubmission of assignments was popular, and approximately half of the students opted to resubmit. Our hope that errors would not be repeated in subsequent assignments was only partially met. We consequently added criteria requiring the incorporation of feedback into the evaluation rubrics.

Provide Multiple Means of Representation

Course content was offered via text, video, and audio resources. Fortunately, content in multiple formats for the weekly readings was readily available under Creative Commons licenses. The availability of closed captioning and transcripts was one of our criteria to ensure that the content was accessible. We used the Moodle settings to require that relevant course content was viewed and assessed with quizzes before coursework could be submitted. Synchronous meetings provided another means of representation of the learning outcomes. These meetings used the web conferencing features of text-based chatting along with the audiovisual delivery of course content.

How Did This Work in Practice?

Creating a UDL-friendly course was limited by what was possible through our institution's implementation of Moodle. We were unable to integrate the course content and quizzes in a manner that allowed students to test their knowledge as they viewed, listened to, or read the content. Instead, their understanding of the material was assessed separately using Moodle quizzes.

In the synchronous meetings, initially, one instructor facilitated the discussion in the course chat box while the other co-instructor lectured. It was an effective way of providing content in different modes, but unfortunately, the dynamic changed when we introduced student presentations. We found it challenging to paraphrase the students' presentations synchronously, without making editorial changes.

Provide Multiple Means of Action and Expression

Students were given options for submitting the topic selection and research log assignments in oral or print form. The course also featured two methods (quizzes and in-class presentations) for students to demonstrate they understood the course content. The weekly quizzes used a randomized question bank and could be repeated three times with a 24-hour delay between attempts to encourage reflection and review of the course materials. Their highest grade was entered as part of the participation grade. Each student was also required to sign up for an in-class presentation that involved the use of course readings to answer questions. Students submitted their slides or notes so that we provided feedback before their presentation dates.

How Did This Work in Practice?

Information literacy in the university context is heavily text-based. Consequently, we struggled with the UDL principle of providing multiple means of action and expression. Most students did not opt to submit assignments in an oral format, but the advantage of UDL-friendly course design is that the option is always there for the one or two students who do. The first term we taught this course, the classes that were not mandatory were unstructured question-and-answer sessions and were not used. In subsequent semesters we required students to sign up for classes. Students who preferred the structure of classes attended weekly. More independent learners chose which synchronous meetings they needed to participate in. Engaged participation worked best when we instituted student presentations based on course content. Student presentations had the benefit of sharing student viewpoints via peer-to-peer learning. We provided a summary at the end of the class so that our role was facilitating and contextualizing a learning environment rather than simply transmitting information.

> **Bottom Line:** We were drawn to UDL as a framework because planning with UDL does not assume a one-size-fits-all approach; instead, it considers the variability of all learners by offering options. Teaching is only one part of the librarian's role at MSVU. Given our time restrictions, our goal was to curate and adapt existing materials to make the course as UDL-friendly as possible by providing as many options as possible.

The UD Paradox

As discussed briefly in the flexible use section earlier, it can be difficult to strike a balance between widest-possible usability and simplicity, especially in unmediated environments. If we aim to "design for all," then we are not really designing for anyone. The breadth of human abilities, conditions, barriers, and their combinations is staggering, and there is no feasible way to consider and design for all of them. A paradox exists wherein it is possible to use universal design principles to create online environments that are too cumbersome and complex for anyone to use, thus negating the effects of the effort altogether. Critics of universal design (e.g., Bringolf, 2008) describe it as an unrealistic utopia, impractical, or a misnomer (confused with inclusive design or accessibility). The faceted nature of universal design, especially when applied to multiple environments, can be confusing and contradictory, making it easy to focus too intently on one audience or barrier at the expense of others. However, within the context of designing environments and services for online library patrons, the foundational elements of UD, and in particular the critical questions that can be applied in each category, are useful in allowing library staff to thoughtfully and deliberately make design decisions that will benefit the majority of their populations. Universal design considerations should be paired with frequent usability testing and other forms of user feedback to determine if the design works as intended. Libraries should also never consider their environments "done" after the design and implementation process is finished. What works for online patrons this year may not work in another year or two, especially when technological advances are happening at such a speedy rate.

Inclusive Practices

This chapter focuses on the design of inclusive environments to ensure equitable services and resources for online patrons. In addition to the technical, legal, and design-focused strategies discussed earlier, intentionally design your online environments using inclusive practices. In particular, we recommend designing your online presence through a critical lens that recognizes that the dominant culture in any environment injects bias into supporting systems. Without utilizing critical evaluation during the design process, you reinforce the ideals of a dominant culture and risk disenfranchising your online patrons. In order to equitably represent the diversity of the communities your library serves, carefully and intentionally craft your language, policies, and services with others in mind. For more on this topic and critical librarianship strategies, see Pagowsky and McElroy's (2016) *Critical Library Pedagogy Handbook*.

Case Study: Using Microsoft Office's Accessibility Checker

Ariana Baker, MLIS, MEd, Distance Learning Librarian, *Coastal Carolina University, Kimbel Library*

I have been posting documents online for many years, but it wasn't until I began teaching online, for-credit classes that I became aware of the importance of universal design. At my institution, when we teach online we are encouraged to enroll in courses through our Center for Teaching Excellence. When I did so, I learned that my documents did not follow best practices in universal design. Specifically, I was told that my lack of page breaks, headings, alternative text, and hyperlink text created a minefield of inaccessibility issues that could potentially impede student learning.

Fortunately, universal design is easier to implement than many people realize. In my Center for Teaching Excellence courses, I learned about an easy-to-use tool that helps make online resources more accessible: the Microsoft Office Accessibility Checker. The purpose is to make documents easily readable by using designated formatting tools. The accessibility checker scans documents and lists items that may be inaccessible. For each item, the checker provides an explanation of the potential problem and how to fix it.

I have gotten into the habit of using the accessibility checker after creating all new Office documents. To do so on a PC, select "File" > "Info" > "Check for Issues" > "Check Accessibility." On a Mac, select "Review" > "Check Accessibility."

After clicking the "Check Accessibility" option, the document is quickly scanned for errors (always inaccessible for people with disabilities), warnings (often inaccessible for people with disabilities), and tips (accessible but suggestions for improvement are available). These errors, warnings, and tips are labeled and linked to the problem location within the document. They are followed by explanations of how the problems affect accessibility and how they can be fixed.

The following are some examples of accessibility problems that I often encounter. They are easily found and fixed using the Microsoft Office Accessibility Checker.

Page Breaks: Rather than pressing enter to get to the bottom of a page, use page breaks instead. That way, a screen reader won't read through every empty line (which may cause users to think they have reached the end of a document) but will instead know to automatically skip to the next page.

Headings: Use official styles instead of bold, italics, and so on to create headings. This allows screen readers to recognize that there is a section heading. Users can then jump within a document to each heading. The use of official style headings also makes it easy to create a table of contents, which can be useful for all users, not only those with low vision.

Alt Text: Use alternative text to explain visual content. Screen readers will read the alternative text for people who cannot see an image so they know what the content is. It is important to be descriptive with alternative text.

Hyperlink Text: Use descriptive language and then hyperlink it, rather than general language such as "click here" or a URL. For example, instead of writing "Click here to learn more about this topic," write "Read this document about accessible Word documents to learn more about this topic." That will provide context to all readers, visually impaired and otherwise, so they can quickly decide if they want to click through.

I now use the accessibility checker before I upload all documents. As universal design becomes the norm rather than the exception, I believe more librarians will be expected to do the same.

Bottom Line: Microsoft Office Accessibility Checker can help us save time and prevent frustration by enabling us to create inclusive, streamlined materials that benefit all users, not only those who require accessibility accommodations.

One Size Doesn't Fit All

Technology has made it possible for many more people to access and interact with online content despite their physical abilities, geographic locations, and other barriers. Tools like screen readers can help those with low vision interact with text content. Voice-activated command systems can help those with mobility or other physical impairments access what they need. And haptic technology can help those with sensory problems experience

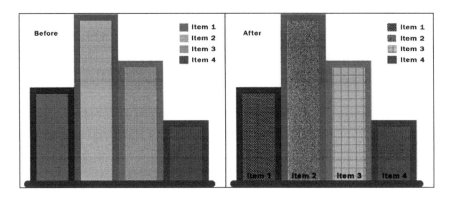

Figure 3.2   Patterns and colors chart for individuals with colorblindness.

their world in new ways. But we are not yet to a place where our technological development can guarantee an equitable experience for our online patrons. Deliberate design plays a critical role in improving the user experience. The negative effects of colorblindness in online environments, for example, can be mitigated through thoughtful and deliberate design. As shown in Figure 3.2, using both shading and shapes or patterns to convey meaning can help information stand out to colorblind users.

Yet, colorblindness is just one of many challenges that our patrons may have to contend with to find and use the information that is readily available to those without those challenges. Check out https://www.usability.gov/ for more tips.

There are many ways to approach the design and creation of library services and resources. How you choose to approach online reference, instruction, discovery, metadata schemas, interlibrary loan policies, and others will vary based on your population, budget, and resources. There will always be a limit to the amount of time, money, and expertise you can employ in your organization, but it is important to do what you can to design your services to accommodate as many patrons as possible. One-size-fits-all is not an approach we employ to serve patrons who visit our physical locations, and it should not be employed to serve online patrons either. By taking the principles of universal design, and more broadly inclusive design, into consideration when designing your online environments, you can mitigate frustrations, improve learning opportunities, and create more equitable access to information not only for your geographically remote patrons but also for anyone who chooses to engage with the library online.

CHAPTER FOUR

Reference for Online Patrons

Jason M. Coleman

Introduction

It is possible to imagine a future in which access to information is so intuitive and productivity tools are so enriched with built-in knowledge of citation styles, copyright law, and instructors' requirements that patrons no longer encounter problems or desire guidance. Since this utopic (or dystopic) day is far away, libraries that wish to see their patrons thrive today must provide assistance for tasks ranging from the mechanics of searching databases to strategies for articulating search queries to the location of the button used for paying a fine.

In Chapter 5 we discuss methods for doing this proactively by delivering guiding information that equips patrons to make more informed choices. Here our focus is on providing guidance at the point of need. We address methods for facilitating connections between patrons and the staff who are trained to help them as well as methods for infusing the knowledge of these staff into online systems so that the answers can be easily found when needed. We also discuss strategies for effectively conducting reference interviews with online patrons. For the purposes of these discussions we use the definition of reference work provided in 2008 by the Reference and User Services Association (RUSA), a division of the American Library Association (ALA). It presents reference work as a broad category that includes, but is not limited to, direct provision of help.

> *Reference transactions* are information consultations in which library staff recommend, interpret, evaluate, or use information resources to help others to meet particular information needs. Reference transactions do not include formal instruction or exchanges that provide assistance with locations, schedules, equipment, supplies, or policy statements.

Reference work includes reference transactions and other activities that involve the creation, management, and assessment of information or research resources, tools, and services.

Guiding Principles

There is no one prescriptive recipe for ensuring that your library is providing its patrons with the best possible reference service. The tremendous variation among libraries and the communities they serve precludes such an approach. We cannot tell you exactly what to do. Instead, we provide a set of guiding principles for online reference services and a wealth of specific projects and technologies libraries have implemented to meet their service quality goals.

American Library Association Guidelines

ALA has published several guidelines and policy statements. The three that are most germane to online reference call for equity and high quality. Its statement on *Access to Digital Information, Services, and Networks* (2009) declares that "digital information, services, and networks provided directly or indirectly by the library should be equally, readily, and equitably accessible to all library users." The ALA's *Standards for Distance Learning Library Services* (2016) call for libraries to provide online learners with services that are equivalent to those available to patrons at physical facilities. They also specify that online learners be given direct access to library personnel who can "facilitat[e] successful use of library resources, particularly electronic resources requiring computer and digital literacy, and information literacy skills" (Library Requirements section, para. 3). And ALA's *Guidelines for Implementing and Maintaining Virtual Reference Services* (2017) state that virtual reference service should have the same "status and quality goals as face-to-face reference" and that all reference services should be of high quality.

Best Practices

These guiding principles will help you achieve this broad vision of high quality, equity, and accessibility for your online reference services.

Avoid Making Assumptions about Your Patrons

When you are in the act of answering a question posed by a specific person or creating online content to assist a hypothetical patron, it can be difficult to avoid imagining a set of life circumstances or motivations for the individual or individuals you are helping. These imagined conditions may lead you to provide information that, while technically correct, is not particularly useful. They also inform decisions about how much detail to provide when describing processes such as interlibrary loan, placing holds, and creating search queries. And perhaps most importantly, they can cause you to leave out some of the options available to our patrons. For example, in the context of online reference, it is common to assume that the patron is far away and unable to visit the physical library. A librarian who makes this assumption may fail to mention highly relevant resources that cannot be delivered remotely or a high-value ancillary service, such as writing assistance, that is only available to onsite patrons.

In order to provide reference assistance that is actually helpful, the individuals who deliver these services should be trained to conduct thorough reference interviews that feature a series of questions designed to elucidate the actual circumstances of the person who is seeking help. Some questions that can be particularly useful when providing reference assistance to online patrons are:

- Are you able to come to the library?
- Are you familiar with our interlibrary loan services?
- Are you familiar with our document delivery services?
- Do you have a deadline for obtaining the information you seek?
- Do you mind if I ask where you are located?

ALA's (2011) *Guidelines for the Behavioral Performance of Reference and Information Service Providers* emphasizes the importance of checking for understanding and asking patrons if their questions have been answered completely. Those two strategies are especially vital in situations where vocal and visual cues are absent, such as e-mail or online chat transactions. When presented sincerely, these invitations to continue the conversation are useful safeguards against the miscommunication that can arise from making assumptions.

When creating online content such as topic overviews, assignment guides, or answers to frequently asked questions, the pressure to write succinctly competes with the goal of addressing as many potential patrons as possible. In libraries that have a large population of local users, this conflict is likely to give rise to content that ignores the realities of online patrons and assumes a reader who can easily make use of location-bound services and resources. You can use several strategies to guard against this oversight:

- Encourage content creators to develop content with an online patron who lives far from the library in mind. In many situations content written explicitly for such an individual will be equally useful for those who have ready access to the physical facility.

- Charge an employee or group of employees with the task of reviewing all reference content and identifying instances where the content is not particularly useful to patrons who can access the library's services and resources only remotely.
- Encourage content providers to routinely add a conspicuous section indicating what, if anything, is different for online patrons. For short content this could be a bolded heading such as "**For online patrons:**" For longer content this could take the form of a separate page or module.
- Invite online users to review specific content and provide feedback about how well it addresses their needs.

Provide Several Options

A patron seeking access to *Jane Eyre* has a wealth of options available to them beyond borrowing your library's copy. The same is true of a patron seeking resources about the origins of Thanksgiving or the future of wind power. Even the patron who wants to cite an article in APA style has options. Indeed, if you think about it, you will recognize that nearly every patron need can be met in a variety of ways.

Well-intentioned librarians will sometimes present only the most popular path to achieving a goal rather than risk annoying a patron with a plethora of alternatives. While this may spare confusion, it can also result in patrons not receiving the help they need. A useful compromise is to provide detail about the options that have worked best for other users and to list a few additional options with an offer to provide additional information about them if requested. This strategy is particularly important when communicating asynchronously through means such as e-mail or posts to online discussions. There are two main reasons. The first is that those formats deny patrons opportunities to use nonverbal cues to convey that the available options are not fully satisfactory. The second is that the time delay inherent to these communications may deny the patron sufficient time to fully explain their situation.

Make It Easy to Obtain Live Help

In many contexts, patrons are more likely to seek library-related help from friends or the Internet than they are from library employees (Estabrook, Witt, & Rainie, 2017). Libraries need to do a better job of promoting their reference services and of making them easy and convenient to use. You should establish and maintain a variety of methods for patrons to obtain help including phone, e-mail, texting, chat, and the option to request appointments that use any of these communication channels or online videos.

All library homepages should include a conspicuous, well-labeled link to live help. Ideally, this link will be placed on all pages on a library's site and embedded in third-party software to which the library subscribes or contributes, including databases, learning management systems (LMS), and content creation platforms such as LibGuides. To make it as easy as possible for patrons to obtain live help, embed chat widgets throughout your site or implement proactive chat systems that provide a clear invitation to chat after a patron has been on a page for a certain amount of time. Consider including names and photos of the individuals who staff these services to help patrons recognize that the service is operated by real people rather than robots and to make it easy for patrons to follow up with questions that occur to them after the live help session has ended.

Investigate the Common Information Needs of Online Patrons

Libraries that lack the resources to provide 24/7 access to enough live help to address the needs of all their users should compensate for this shortfall by designing their site and discovery tools to be as intuitive as possible, creating online guides or systems to help users find databases or sites appropriate to their needs, and presenting easy-to-follow instructions for using services and products.

Rather than guess at what information to place online and where and how to display it, use direct and indirect evidence about the challenges online users are likely to encounter and the resources they are most likely to need. A record of reference transactions presented by online patrons is an invaluable source of information about ways in which your library's website and discovery tools may be failing to present information as clearly as intended. Periodically review this record to identify frequently encountered obstacles and then either modify your services to remove the obstacles or develop online aids to help patrons circumvent them.

When the solution is to develop aids or workarounds, place links to them as close to the point of need as possible. For example, if your patrons are confused about which link to use in your catalog to request a hold and renaming the link is not possible, you could develop an online aid with an explanation of which link to click. A link to the aid should be placed near the set of links available to patrons in the catalog. Failing that, it could be positioned in a conspicuous position that every user is likely to see (such as near the search button).

Transaction records are extremely helpful, but they do not represent the needs of individuals who are not aware of services or are not willing to contact the library for help. Search logs and web analytics data can give some insight into misunderstandings or errors encountered by a broad population of patrons. These should be examined regularly to identify common topics, services, and resources patrons are searching for and variations in spelling. This knowledge can then be used to add additional metadata to facilitate access, to move access points to key services so they are more obvious, or to rename services. For example, if search logs for your site's search function show that several individuals have entered distance library services as search terms, and the information page you provide about those services uses the phrase "services for online users," you could retitle the page to services for online or distance users.

Neither search logs nor reference transaction records provide information about what services and tools patrons would like to have available to them. For that evidence, it is best to directly ask your online patrons. Surveys, focus groups, and interviews are well suited for gathering general feedback as well as suggestions about how to improve services. We (Bonella, Pitts, & Coleman, 2017) conducted a survey that gave insights we used to redesign our library's informational pages for distance patrons. In addition to providing opportunities for open-ended feedback, we listed the services our library provides for online learners and asked respondents to indicate which they had used and which they were aware of. We then used information about lack of awareness of key services, such as free delivery of the library's books, to design and implement a promotional campaign. See more details about this in Chapter 8.

In addition to these direct sources of information about the needs, desires, and frustrations of online users, gather insight from indirect sources such as faculty, community organizations, educational surveys, and government agencies. For academic libraries, information about research assignments is a rich source of evidence about questions online students are likely to have. Use this knowledge to develop informational aids tied to these specific assignments. For public libraries, information about legislation being considered in outlying communities as well as demographic data can be used to create resource guides that anticipate likely inquiries (see Chapter 10). Libraries of all types should also leverage the insights and work of their peers by examining their websites and adapting or linking to their resources that are likely to be of use to their online population.

Resolve to Make a Difference

Reference work can be incredibly rewarding, but at times it can be stressful and exhausting. Some users will send inappropriate messages. Some will demand a level of service that is too resource intensive. And when a system goes offline, a flood of questions may follow. At times like that, you and your employees might find empathy and patience in short supply and might wish to provide short, not particularly helpful replies. Or you might chastise or admonish your users. In online settings it is especially vital that you not engage in this behavior. Too often, what is perceived as rudeness or laziness ends up being a result of miscommunications stemming from cultural differences or lack of language skills. A patron treated unfairly is likely to relate their experience to many others. However, when you give the benefit of the doubt and discover that what you perceived as a prank question (e.g., Do you have books about love?) was an earnest one, you may end up making a tremendous difference in the course of multiple lives.

One of the fundamental tensions in reference work is that between giving patrons quick and efficient answers and teaching them new skills and perspectives. While both are laudable, the latter is more likely to have a lasting, transformative impact. When training employees to deliver service to patrons, encourage them to look for opportunities to empower patrons to become more independent. For example, when a patron asks whether your library owns a particular book, rather than simply giving the answer, ask the patron if they would like to learn how to find the answer themselves. Some might decline, but a number will eagerly accept the invitation, especially when it is given kindly and sincerely.

Expressing kindness and looking for opportunities to teach are two ways to make a difference. Another is a determination to advocate on behalf of online users (see Chapter 9). In the course of answering questions presented by online users, it is likely that you and your employees will identify a number of policies or design decisions that deny these users access that is equivalent to that available to local users. Lack of access to collections of textbooks, reference materials, and special collections is a common example. Rather than accept the status quo as fixed, take the opportunity to explore whether other libraries like yours have discovered workarounds. It may be that new technologies that will enable you to adhere to the law, protect materials, and unlock all of your library's resources for your patrons have evolved. If you continually run up against barriers when you try to advocate for online users, invite the key decision makers in your library to join you in an offsite meeting and present them with a series of authentic tasks you know online users are trying to perform. Or if this is too bold, ask online users if you can conduct user testing in which you record them as they perform common tasks. Firsthand exposure to the barriers your online users are encountering is likely to make a much greater impression than reports and anecdotes ever will.

Building Your Service Portfolio

Your patrons have a wide variety of information needs that vary in complexity, topic, and urgency. Some will have access to a number of technologies, and a wide array of times they can seek out answers. Others will be quite limited in one or more of these areas. In order to meet the diverse reference needs of your online patrons, your portfolio of services must also feature diversity. You need to create services that connect patrons directly to reference personnel and that are designed to route questions to appropriate experts. At the same time, you need to embed answers and advice directly into the systems your patrons use. In this section we describe core and optional services in both categories.

Case Study: Virtual Consultations

Lindley Homol, MLIS, MEd, Manager of Global Campus
Engagement and Online Learning, *Northeastern University Library*

Background

In June 2016, I took over as the liaison to our university's Education program. This program was comprised of students at the doctoral and master's levels, and the learners were primarily online students. To accommodate the subject-specific and specialized research needs of these students, the library had been offering a research consultation service. Students could book a one-on-one appointment with their liaison librarian, either in person or over the phone.

Because many of the students in the Education program could not participate in an in-person appointment, their only option was a phone call. Doing a research consultation over the phone, especially one that involved searching in a few different databases, was not ideal. Much of the time was spent making sure the student and librarian were on the same page, and trying to explain the mechanics of a complicated search statement was problematic. Without being able to see each other, or each other's computer screens, it was difficult to ensure mutual understanding of the research problem and potential solutions.

Solution

For the fall 2016 quarter, I began offering web conference consultations so that online learners would have more options when selecting their research help experience. Web conferences would allow me to share my screen for database and search demonstrations, and both the student and I could use our webcams to talk face to face. Students were able to book an online consultation directly through the Education Research LibGuide for their program, using Springshare's LibCal software. When completing the appointment request, they received options of how they would like to meet with me: in person, over the phone, or via web conference. Students who selected a web conference would receive a follow-up e-mail from me, with a link to my personal web conference meeting room. I used the BlueJeans meeting platform, which was already available through an institutional subscription. Thus, it cost nothing to offer this new service to students.

How It Helped

These web conferences provided several benefits for online students. First, the ability to share computer screens better approximated the in-person consultation experience by allowing the student and me to work through a search together. By allowing us to view the same screen, web conferences helped to cut down on the confusion and troubleshooting that often took place over the phone. Second, the web conference format provided flexibility. I could conduct the consultation from any computer with an Internet connection, which made scheduling off-hours consultations easier. Third, by allowing the student and me to see each other, the web conferences could promote a more personal connection to the library for the student.

Results and Future Plans

In the first month of the fall quarter, 20 consultations were scheduled, and 11 of them were booked as web conferences (55 percent). By the end of the winter quarter, 28 web conference consultations had been scheduled, out of 86 total consultations (33 percent). When the average length of consultations was compared, in-person appointments averaged 37 minutes, web conferences averaged 36, and telephone consultations averaged 27. The difference between the length of in-person or web conference consultations and telephone appointments was statistically significant. This is one indication that the web conference consultations better approximated the in-person consultation experience than telephone appointments did. The initial popularity of the web conference option among Education students has resulted in plans for other liaison librarians to begin offering this service to their students in the next academic year.

Considerations

Although virtual consultations proved popular with some online graduate students, not all students may feel comfortable meeting with a librarian via web conference. I worked with a program of adult learners in which online office hours were part of the department's culture, so these students may have been more comfortable with this option than others, such as undergraduates. I also found promotion of the virtual consultation option to be crucial—students had to first know the option existed in order to take advantage of it. While I promoted the option mainly through the LibGuide associated with the program, additional possibilities for promotion include online classrooms or student newsletters. Finally, when selecting the technology to use to deliver the consultations, I selected an option that put little burden on the student. I reasoned that if students were required to download software or create an account to use the service, they might be less likely to schedule an appointment.

Bottom Line: Web conference consultations can be a low-cost and effective way to connect with online students.

Connecting Patrons to Reference Personnel

Patrons have questions, and your library employees have the wisdom, experience, and desire needed to get them to the answers they need. Unless your patrons are quite unusual, a good portion of them expect immediate answers and are not willing to spend much time or effort trying to figure out how to reach your library employees. Your challenge is to make the availability of help obvious, the means to reaching it simple, and the choices of times and connection methods plentiful. Fortunately there are several strategies for meeting these challenges.

Core Services

There are a wealth of technologies that help people communicate at a distance. Choose a combination that will appeal to the full spectrum of ages and technological aptitude within your community of patrons. Ensure that your constellation of service offerings can facilitate one-to-one, one-to-many, and many-to-many connections. And wherever possible, give your patrons choices about whom to contact, when to make contact, and how to do so.

Communication technologies. Employ communication technologies that are in wide use by your patrons. Offer all of the following:

- **E-mail.** Provide at least one e-mail address to patrons. Ideally your library will monitor this address frequently and provide an initial reply within a few hours of the time the e-mail is received. If your library is large and has teams of employees who answer specific types of questions, create e-mail addresses for those teams and make them available directly to patrons too. In addition to e-mail addresses, create an online form that generates an e-mail and prompts patrons to provide essential details about themselves and their information needs. Patrons can be given options about which of your service groups their question should go to.

- **Phone.** Provide your patrons with the phone numbers for each of your library's major service points.
- **Online chat.** If your budget allows, subscribe to a full-featured chat service such as Libraryh3lp, Question Point, LibAnswers, or Refchatter. These services enable multiple individuals to monitor incoming chats and make it easy to transfer chats among operators. Many offer extra features such as canned messages that can be used to speed up and standardize responses, auto-replies when the service is busy, proactive invitations to chat that are triggered after a patron spends a prescribed amount of time on a page, methods for operators to chat with each other, widget design tools, and much more. Some have extra service tiers that allow you to connect your patrons to individuals from other libraries at times when your staff is not available. The market changes frequently so make sure to look for up-to-date information about service options before you select a product for your institution. RUSA's Virtual Reference Companion (http://www.ala.org/rusa/vrc) is a resource with advice and links to resources that can help you make a wise choice.
- **Texting.** Some online chat services include a method for routing incoming texts to the chat service. If this is not available, consider acquiring a smartphone that receives the text messages. Make this phone available at your general service point or establish a schedule for passing the phone among reference employees.

Appointments. While real-time, point-of-need help will meet the needs of many patrons, others will benefit more from prescheduled appointments. These arrangements may be particularly beneficial to novice researchers or individuals with complex research questions. Use one or more of the following options for setting up appointments:

- **Menu-based scheduling.** Present patrons with a list of individuals who are available for appointments. At a minimum this list should include brief descriptions of areas of expertise and contact information. The onus is then on patrons to contact one or more of those individuals to request an appointment.
- **Mediated scheduling.** Provide your patrons with a general contact who will communicate with them to gather information about their topic and their preferred meeting times and then schedule a session with a library employee who has matching expertise and availability. If possible, create a web form that prompts patrons to provide the essential details the main contact person or service point needs to make a match.

- **Direct scheduling through sign-up.** The simplest method for patrons is to provide them with the ability to see available time slots for each individual employee and to select one of those slots. To ensure that the list of available time slots is updated dynamically, use a web application that can link with each individual employee's online calendar. Popular options include Spring-share's LibCal, Doodle, schedule.me, and youcanbook.me. The case studies in this chapter by Lindley Homol and Jennifer Rundels illustrate how LibCal can be used to facilitate connections between patrons and experts.

Additional Services

Once you have all of these core services in place, identify user groups that are not taking advantage of your online reference services and implement additional options that might appeal to them. The following are a few that will broaden your reach and capacity to deliver help. Each of these can be used by a general service point or by individual librarians who have appointments with patrons.

- **Social media.** Your library can create reference service accounts on several communication platforms, including Facebook, SnapChat, and Twitter. Make sure to investigate the privacy options available on each platform and clearly indicate to patrons which communications will be visible by the public. As with the more traditional core of services, a quick response time is essential. Do not provide a service unless you have sufficient resources to ensure an initial reply quickly, ideally within one business day.
- **Web conferencing.** Platforms such as Adobe Connect, GoToMeeting, or Zoom are useful for conducting online reference consultations. These platforms provide visuals, such as live video and screen sharing, that can expedite and enhance communications about complicated processes. General reference services can also employ this technology for point-of-need help.
- **Group or community blogs/forums.** In academic or school settings library employees can use the discussion board or blog within an LMS as a place for students to post questions about research. Answers shared in this manner become available to all members of the class. The same general approach can be used with other groups through means such as public reference blogs on the library's website or on newspaper's website.
- **Coedited online documents.** In educational settings, especially those where students are expected to document their development over time, library employees can interact directly with patrons through shared documents. Productivity suites such as Google Apps or Microsoft's Office 365 make it simple to control who can access and edit individual documents or groups of documents within folders. A librarian could take a question a patron poses and post both it and the answer to a document that is shared with the patron. The patron could then reply within the document to create a record of the interaction. With the patron's permission, the librarian could also share the

document with colleagues and invite them to augment the conversation with their insights. Used systematically, this approach could result in an individual patron possessing several documents over time that record the growth of their information literacy knowledge.

Case Study: A Model for Engaging Students with Online Research Consultations

Jennifer J. Rundels, MLIS, MA, Assistant Professor, Library Research and Instruction Services, *Central Michigan University*

This case study describes a model for appointment-based reference that uses videoconferencing and screen-sharing technology to engage students during online consultations. Online research consultations are personalized, interactive sessions that provide online students the same level of service that on-campus students receive during face-to-face consultations. Since February 2016, students near and far—from small towns in Michigan to military bases in Germany—have benefited from this reference model. Regardless of their physical location, students are getting the research help they need to be successful.

Initially, research consultations were promoted to on-campus students who could presumably meet face to face for personalized research assistance. However, some on-campus students expressed a preference for meeting online. Technology has made it possible to accommodate these students—and online students as well—without sacrificing service. In fact, the face-to-face experience has been replicated online.

At first, students requested consultations through e-mail that required multiple e-mail responses to coordinate appointment times. This proved to be extremely time consuming. Eventually, Springshare's LibCal Appointment Scheduler was used to automate the scheduling process. Online appointment forms were synced to Outlook and customized to generate confirmation e-mails and appointment reminders. I found that when setting up availability times, I needed to consider how many hours I wanted to devote to consultations each day or week and make myself available for those hours only. Otherwise, I would have been overwhelmed with back-to-back appointments. This revolving-door scenario was initially a reality for me.

I have found that demonstrating the research process using each student's research topic has been instrumental to the success of this model. However, the ability of students to participate in the research process is equally important. The use of videoconferencing and screen-sharing technology has ensured that online research consultations have been just as interactive and engaging as face-to-face consultations. Various videoconferencing tools can be used to successfully administer online research consultations, including Zoom, join.me, and WebEx. Initially, I used Zoom because of its ease-of-use and intuitive interface. But now I use WebEx exclusively since the university's Office of Information Technology has discouraged the use of cloud-based software as a security measure. Although Zoom proved to be much more intuitive for both students and librarians alike, WebEx also gets the job done. Using WebEx just takes a bit more troubleshooting when students have trouble enabling their audio, which happens somewhat frequently. Although some are more intuitive than others, any videoconferencing and screen-sharing tool makes it possible for online students to participate in the process to the same degree as their on-campus counterparts.

The model for engaging students with online consultations incorporates several key steps in the research process:

1. Navigating the university libraries' website to locate journal article databases;
2. Constructing search strategies using Boolean operators, truncation, and nesting to locate relevant articles on student-driven, assignment-based topics;
3. Refining search results to locate scholarly and peer-reviewed articles within required date ranges;
4. Evaluating search results; and
5. Marking records for citation generation.

At the beginning of every online research consultation, I conduct an informal reference interview to develop rapport and gain a better understanding of the student's topic. When students present topics that are too broad or narrow in scope, I suggest adjustments as necessary. Next, I direct the student's attention to my shared screen, which is typically the library's homepage. From there, I navigate to a recommended database and begin discussing the creation of a search strategy. This is a great time to introduce students to Boolean operators, truncation, and nesting.

I believe the success of this model can be attributed to the fact that I never "over prepare" for a consultation. In other words, I never use canned searches. Instead, I demonstrate how to adjust my initial search strategy after reviewing my initial search results. I am not afraid if the first few attempts are not perfect. I allow students to see the process as it unfolds. This demonstrates that even librarians have to tweak their search strategies as they go. I have discovered that this demystifies the process and builds student confidence.

Next, I demonstrate how to refine search results by source type and date range before scrolling through the results and previewing article abstracts. I always encourage students to participate in the evaluation process by asking them to indicate which articles appear most useful. I mark the articles they choose and export them to a citation manager, such as EndNote, to format the citations. Finally, I cut and paste the citations into a Word document where I also include the search strategies used, along with links to the databases searched. This is the student's takeaway. Before e-mailing the takeaway document to the student, I show the student how to access the articles from the Word document just created. I never assume students know how link resolvers work.

Before ending each consultation, I ask students if the consultation was helpful and what they thought was most useful. I have discovered that most students offer feedback during the course of the consultation itself. One hour after the consultation has ended, the student receives a short survey. LibCal makes it easy to automate the process of gathering feedback.

Positive feedback among students has routinely generated consultation requests from students' peers while also impacting faculty perception. For example, one faculty member required that all of the students in his online courses schedule a research consultation with me. He stated in an e-mail, "My current MSA 698 students just gave their presentations the past two Tuesdays during our chat. Almost all of them mentioned your name personally as being the greatest helper in getting their 698 project completed. That made me feel good and it should make you feel great." The administrators of that same graduate degree program identified research consultations with a librarian as a best practice for student success.

Ultimately I attribute the overwhelming success of online research consultations to three main factors: (1) enthusiastic promotion of one-on-one research consultations during library instruction sessions, (2) supportive faculty who encourage students to schedule appointments with me, and (3) word of mouth among satisfied students and their peers.

Bottom Line: How can librarians conduct effective, engaging research consultations for the growing online student population? Is it possible to replicate the face-to-face research consultation in an online environment? Using videoconferencing and screen-sharing technology to engage students can demystify the research process.

Embedding Help at the Point of Need

Imagine the entire set of questions all of your patrons have as they interact with your library and its resources. Doubtless this set contains a number of highly specific and unique questions that it would be quite difficult for your staff to anticipate. However, much of the set probably consists of frequently repeated, basic questions, such as "when is the library open?" or "can I download eBooks?" and less frequently repeated, slightly more complex questions such as "what is the process for requesting a book chapter through interlibrary loan?" or "how do I limit my search to reports of the results of empirical studies?"

When you can anticipate questions and answer them clearly and accurately for an imagined patron, place the answers online where you expect your patrons to be hunting for them. This will spare them the frustration of being stuck at a time when they are unable or unwilling to try to contact a library employee. It will also spare your employees from answering the same set of questions over and over.

Core Services

One of the reasons libraries have websites is to deliver answers to common questions so that patrons can find them wherever they are and whenever they want the answer. The answers to the most common questions are usually provided on or linked directly from the homepage. More specific common questions are often addressed through topically organized subpages. In addition to using the core of your website to proactively answer questions, enhance your site with the following features:

- **FAQ section.** Create a specific section in your site for presenting answers to frequently asked questions. At its simplest this can be a single page with question and answer pairs. Through use of software such as Springshare's LibAnswers or Libraryh3lp, it can also be a searchable set of question/answer pairs that can be tagged and categorized. FAQ sets require ongoing maintenance and analysis. See Warner and Pierard's case study in this chapter for an example.
- **Instructional videos.** When answering questions that involve executing a series of specific, nonintuitive steps on a website, provide short narrated videos with captions. These videos can be linked from the point of need and can also be presented as a collection on the library website. For maximum success, limit the length of a video to 30 seconds. Since it is likely that these videos will become obsolete quickly, having short videos will make maintenance easier.
- **Topic pages.** If you notice that several of your questions are related to a common topic (e.g., genealogy, small businesses, and citation styles), create a webpage that provides general information about the topic and simultaneously answers some of the most common questions you have received about it. If your library plans to develop several topic pages, we recommend that

you create a clear organizational scheme and develop a set of design standards. And rather than try to re-create Wikipedia, we suggest basing your efforts on evidence about what your patrons are seeking. Search logs, focus groups, reference transaction logs, and statistics about resource use can all be helpful.

- **Assignment pages.** Libraries serving students should pay close attention to the questions they are asking related to specific classes or assignments. If there are several questions about the same assignment, contact the instructor to learn about the goals of the assignment and how the library can help students succeed. In addition to directly benefiting students, these pages help library employees who may be fielding questions about a wide variety of courses.

Case Study: Bringing the Library to the Students with LibGuides LTI Integration

Sandra Calemme McCarthy, MSLS, MA, Faculty Librarian, *Washtenaw Community College, Richard D. Bailey Library*

Background

Washtenaw Community College (WCC) located in Ann Arbor, Michigan, has an full-time equivalent enrollment of approximately 8,000 students who take online, blended, and face-to-face courses. Online courses at WCC experienced a 25 percent growth during the 2016–2017 academic year.

One goal of the Bailey Library at WCC is to provide unlimited access to all of its electronic resources through the Blackboard learning management system. The surge of available e-resources and the shift to greater use of them by all academic areas has necessitated a strengthening of access through Blackboard.

The Problem

Over 75 percent of faculty at WCC used Blackboard, yet the library's limited presence there restricted access to e-resources integral to academic success. We realized that the library should become embedded in Blackboard.

The Solution

The library had subscribed to Springshare's LibGuides product since 2010. In 2016, librarians investigated the learning tools interoperability

(LTI) functionality offered by LibGuides CMS. LTI functioned as a mediator between LibGuides and Blackboard to embed guides for students. Many course guides had already been created in collaboration with faculty since 2010. At WCC the most-used guides were those that were related to course assignments. In July 2016, the library upgraded to Lib-Guides CMS, which included the LTI functionality, and began setting up the LTI integration.

The integration of LibGuides into Blackboard courses has provided students with access to high-quality information curated by a librarian for the specific course or discipline, point-of-need reference help from a librarian through 24/7 chat or e-mail follow-up, and contact with a subject liaison librarian for research assistance.

The Application of the Solution

There are two options for the LibApps LTI Tool Builder: (1) LTI Automagic or (2) LTI Manual Mode. As the distance learning librarian, I selected the LTI Automagic option because this option made it possible to set up the tool once and then use it in all Blackboard courses.

There were several steps to set up the LibApps LTI Tool Builder. The first step is to enable the LTI Course Page Builder that involves global settings such as content display behavior. The content display behavior specified the logic used to determine which individual LibGuides were displayed in a given Blackboard course. In cases where the matching logic did not identify any specific LibGuides, Bailey Library LibGuide was displayed by default. This generic LibGuide included information about e-resources, services, and how to contact a librarian. The next step was to set up the LTI parameter name. We selected "context_label" to indicate that the course number in Blackboard should be used. Our last step was to add metadata to LibGuides in order to enable communication with Blackboard courses. Once the LTI Tool Builder had been set up in Lib-Guides, the Blackboard technologist set up the LTI Automagic tool configuration details in Blackboard.

Example

The LibGuide for Academic and Career Services course, ACS 108 Critical Reading and Thinking, is a good example of the integration process.

I applied custom metadata to ensure that this LibGuide would appear in the appropriate course in Blackboard.

Within the Blackboard course, students who clicked on the library menu item would then see a link to the appropriate LibGuide.

The Results

After completing the setup, librarians began a campaign to reach out to faculty who had a course guide already created that aligned with a course assignment. This project opened new opportunities for faculty-librarian communication and collaboration to make high-quality information readily available to students.

I also met with the Online Learning, Educational & Media Technology Services Department to set up an agreement on how to move forward with the new tool. We agreed that all new Blackboard courses would include the LTI Automagic setup. I would provide faculty with instructions and would be the key point of reference for all faculty on the LibGuides tool.

At the end of the winter 2017 semester, statistics for course guides were reviewed. For courses that had implemented the Automagic LTI Tool, usage increased from the fall 2016 semester by 23 percent. The next phase in this project will be to continue to contact instructors of other online courses with a research component and work with them to create new course guides to embed in Blackboard. This project will continue to grow as the librarians work with new faculty to bring the library to their students.

Bottom Line: LibGuides CMS LTI functionality, when integrated with Blackboard, provides access to the library's e-resources to support student research.

Additional Services

The techniques discussed earlier are relatively low-tech and easy to apply. They will not, however, answer all of the common questions your patrons have. The information can be difficult to find, and some patrons may not even know that the information exists. Fortunately there are additional strategies that can be employed to address those barriers.

- **Adwords.** Many search platforms provide the ability to present specific information whenever a patron searches for a certain keyword or set of keywords. This is especially valuable when performed on your site's main search box or on the search interface for your catalog or discovery tool. Examine your search logs and then perform the most common searches yourself. When you do so, check to see if the top few results are the ones you suspect the patron is trying to find. In cases where the top results seem unhelpful, consider turning the query into an adword to force a different target to the top of the list of results.

- **Proactive e-mails.** Academic library employees who have been working with online patrons for a few years have likely developed an ability to anticipate the difficulties they will encounter. Rather than wait for those patrons to experience those difficulties, they could send them short e-mails or texts to point them to useful resources such as assignment or topic guides. In other instances, your employees may notice that a patron is having trouble finding information or is requesting materials they could obtain for themselves online. These are opportunities to reach out to the patron to offer assistance and to point them to instructional resources they may not have known exist. For example, if your interlibrary services staff notice that a patron is consistently requesting articles that are available for free online, they could e-mail that patron and kindly explain how to find the materials.
- **Embedding help in an LMS.** Many libraries have a wealth of online guides, videos, and FAQs that provide concise, easily understood instructions. Often these materials receive far less use than the individuals who created them feel they should. A major reason is, of course, that patrons who might benefit from the information are unaware of the fact that it exists, or they are aware, but are unwilling to expend the effort to search for it on websites that are sometimes unwieldy. One way to circumvent this problem is to place the information in front of patrons in places we know they attend to closely. For academic libraries, the LMS is a particularly fruitful point of contact. We recommend that academic libraries contact the individuals who manage the LMS at their institution and explore possibilities for automatically embedding links to course guides and other library content within courses. Some of the vendors librarians use for course guides have developed management tools that allow for automatic integration with some popular systems. See the McCarthy case study in this chapter for an example. But even if this is not a possibility for your library, you can urge your library employees to contact course instructors with requests to place valuable content directly in the LMS.
- **Banks of answers provided previously.** The more curious or ambitious patrons you serve might benefit from combing through banks of anonymized questions and answers provided by your library employees. This is especially true if the patrons can search the bank or browse it by categories. In situations where a librarian works with a specific course, the students could be given access to a bank of questions that were answered for students in the same class in earlier semesters.
- **Moderated discussion boards or forums.** Your library could provide an online forum or discussion board for patrons to pose questions and receive answers that can be viewed by everyone. These forums or boards could be opened up to allow other members of the community to provide answers. While this approach is a natural fit for students in a specific course, it could also be used for broader groups. If you implement this approach, we recommend that you assign at least one library employee as a moderator who can delete spam and inflammatory posts and who can also chime in to provide a library voice when information is presented that is of dubious value.

Case Study: Supporting Online Users with a Frequently Asked Questions Knowledge Base

Adrienne Warner, MLS, First-Year Experience Librarian
Cindy Pierard, MLS, Director of Access Services and
Undergraduate Engagement
The University of New Mexico

Background and Context

New Mexico is a large and rural state, and the University of New Mexico's (UNM) distance education programs have grown steadily. As of 2017, online courses generated more than 48,000 student credit hours for the university, with nearly 9,800 students participating in at least one online course offering. UNM students may concurrently enroll in online and face-to-face classes, and may take classes on more than one UNM campus. This means that students may have multiple roles as on-campus or distance learners with both roles having a possible online component.

Like many libraries, UNM University Libraries (UNMUL) on the main campus has expanded reference services beyond the physical library to include redefining subject librarian positions to emphasize outreach; embedding reference services within academic departments and campus centers; and offering multiple modes of help through chat, phone, e-mail, and text. After roughly a decade of redefining services, we needed to gauge what was working well and what needed improvement. When the UNMUL moved to a new software vendor for our online help services in 2016, the new reference and information services coordinator and her team reviewed existing help services and prioritized the development of a frequently asked questions (FAQ) knowledge base.

Using Search Logs to Develop a New Knowledge Base

The first challenge was considering what to do with existing FAQs. Like many libraries, UNMUL has long included FAQs on our website. Over time, the combination of frequent service changes and staff turnover took its toll on this well-intentioned resource, resulting in a collection of questions, some of which were no longer frequently asked or effectively answered.

The reference team believed it was important to build on existing work, but wanted to go forward with a more responsive model. We decided to incorporate existing FAQs into the new knowledge base but determined that future FAQs would be based on actual user searches.

This approach has necessitated careful monitoring of the search log. Not all terms entered into the search box warrant the creation of a new FAQ. Some are too vague to discern a question, such as a single search for *Japan*. Conversely, narrowly focused searches, such as *history of drug addicted babies*, are so specific that the use by multiple searchers is unlikely. The search log must be considered holistically, however; and multiple queries about a narrowly focused topic may suggest need beyond a single user. The log is archived in its entirety for such longitudinal analysis.

Regular review of the log not only informs the creation of new FAQs but also offers insight into possible FAQ expansion. For instance, information about accessible parking was added to the parking FAQ, along with links to services for users with disabilities after noting several searches for terms such as *handicapped*, *handicap*, *disability*, and *parking*. In this way, FAQs can be responsive to specific searches, while also encouraging discovery of complementary services (e.g., availability of accessible parking along with other library services).

As individual question and answer pairs were created, the reference team also defined attributes for the knowledge base. Our software allows for tagging FAQs with topics and keywords, and the reference team initially created a set of broad, controlled-vocabulary topics. Each FAQ is assigned at least one topic, allowing for discovery through specific searches or broad topics. Although the use of topics was embraced, the team initially did not assign additional keywords. Software limitations prevent wildcard searching, so tagging keywords was cumbersome to perform and resulted in a cluttered external-facing keyword list. The team later reversed that decision when we realized that keywords help with matching FAQs to natural language terms.

The log is instrumental in FAQ creation, but we are cautious about using it to draw too many conclusions. For example, a call number entered into the search box may simply be an error—the user may have intended to search the catalog. Another challenge we noticed early on was that any directions included within the search box must be very clear. The terms originally placed inside the FAQ search box (*Enter search terms here*) proved to be too vague. The log revealed that some searches typed into the FAQ search box indicated that users were expecting to get human response to what they had typed. Our prompt now reads: *Type here to search FAQs—for more help, chat/email us below*.

Interpreting logs is not foolproof, and we have found it is insufficient to analyze search terms alone. Instead, we conduct search log reviews using search terms together with elements such as timestamp and IP address. For example, multiple searches of similar topics from the same IP address with sequential timestamps help us to see patterns of a single user and their search behavior. This in turn helps us to see patterns that may be beneficially addressed in a new or rewritten FAQ.

Establishing Tone and Style

The reference team had noted the diversity in tone used throughout in previously written FAQs and decided to work toward consistency with tone and style, emphasizing short phrases, bullets, and white space. We developed style guidelines so multiple authors could create consistent FAQs while dividing the creation workload across team members. We developed link-naming and placement conventions for the text and appended links to manage relevant, value-added content. We link to other reference material, such as guides and tutorials, whenever possible, but write enough content on the answer page to answer the question at hand.

Even with guidelines in place, the resultant FAQs had a range of style interpretations and voices, and each FAQ had to be rewritten by one person. In addition, when appropriate, FAQs were written to maximize access for online students—whether local or distant—and to emphasize use of online tools and services. At this point, all FAQs are created by the same person to ensure consistency of tone, style, audience focus, and overall user experience. While this approach may seem limiting, one advantage is the ability to easily edit or delete content that is no longer accurate or useful, allowing us to focus on the current concerns of our users. Joint editorship from a shared account may balance responsibility and maximize agility, and could be a sustainable approach as our knowledge base grows.

Developing a Maintenance Strategy

The reference team uses a multipronged approach to maintain the content of each of the FAQs in the knowledge base. Scheduled maintenance occurs after the end of the fall and spring semesters, with reference team members sharing the load and reviewing all content and links.

Because change is a constant in online library environments, updates to FAQ content are necessary between the periods of scheduled maintenance. The challenge of keeping abreast of all website changes is mitigated by regular internal communication between working groups and commitment to making on-the-fly content edits.

The reference team also plans for FAQ content change. Large-scale changes to the library website or resources are communicated in advance, supporting planning for FAQ updates. At the time of this writing, UNMUL is implementing a new discovery system. The reference and information services coordinator can create FAQs pertaining to the new discovery system, and the FAQ management software allows for questions to remain unpublished (non-discoverable publicly) or published on a specific date (discoverable).

The final prong in the maintenance strategy is to update topic and keyword metadata. Changes to topic titles have been made to reflect natural language use and avoid jargon. For example, *Technology/Equipment* was renamed the more straightforward *Computers/Equipment*. Recently, the team began including topic clouds and related FAQs on each individual answer page, to increase discoverability. As the number of questions in the knowledge base grows, the reference team will continue to monitor the number of questions assigned to each topic, anticipating that splitting topics may be likely.

Understanding Use and Usefulness

With over 4,500 views in its first year, it is clear that the new FAQ knowledge base is contributing to overall reference services. But are the parts as good as the whole? The reference team is using the following metrics in conducting our assessment of what is used and what is useful.

Although we did not initially archive FAQ questions when we went live, we do now so that trend analysis is possible. Use is of particular importance. Most FAQs are viewed multiple times per month, but some are rarely used. We developed criteria for baseline use to keep the knowledge base free from questions that are infrequently asked, deciding that FAQs must have four views within a one-year period of being publicly available. Something we have decided not to worry about is who does the asking, recognizing that FAQs may help library staff as well as our users. We have resolved that who the users are is not as important as the fact that there is use.

We also review the relationship between search terms entered and FAQs retrieved. More than 50 percent of user searches in our knowledge base result in the user clicking a particular FAQ, which is what we hope to see. The mystery lies in understanding those searches that do not result in FAQ clicks even when there appears to be a connection between the search terms and the FAQ language. Another problem is how to interpret cases where users conduct multiple searches for the same or similar terms despite the existence of correlating FAQs. We can see these unmatched queries but are not sure what they are telling us. More study is needed to better understand such patterns.

In addition to reviewing user behavior after the initial FAQ search, we attempt to determine where users are located when conducting searches.

We have used the search log to collect a random sample of IP addresses and found that 20 percent of queries came from servers located outside a 50-mile radius of the main campus, initially suggesting that distant users may be using the FAQ knowledge base. However, IP address may not correlate to user location, since remote servers can be utilized by patrons to maintain privacy online and patrons may be conducting searches from more than one location. Where appropriate, we have sustained a focus on services that need not be accessed in person, such as access to subscription databases from off-campus, ensuring that the information provided is of assistance to both local and online students.

Something that has reinforced our feelings about the usefulness of the FAQ knowledge base is the data on when it is used. Instead of looking only at searches that occur when we are closed and unable to help in other ways, we decided to also examine searches that occurred when other help services (chat, phone, etc.) were available. We were surprised to find that the overwhelming majority of use (75 percent) occurred when users had other options. This suggests that the FAQs are a help mode that users like to have available whether it is the only way they seek to resolve questions or one option among many. The choice is one that our users are clearly exercising.

Bottom Line: Help your online users help themselves with FAQ creation, maintenance, and efficacy analysis.

Champion Your Services and Your Employees

In order to sustain enthusiasm for doing the sometimes hard, and yes, sometimes tedious work required to provide meaningful help to patrons, the managers of your library's reference services will need to make concerted efforts to support the employees who do this work and trumpet the impact they are making. Among the most helpful means of doing this are:

- Collect and share all of the thank-yous, accolades, and statements of gratitude presented by patrons who receive help. Occasionally present these in a public forum such as an all-staff meeting.
- Establish an award for best reference service employee of the year. If possible, make this a monetary award and have a public celebration of this employee. For added impact, try to have some of the patrons who benefitted from this employee's work attend the ceremony and provide testimonials.
- Reach out to the individuals in your library who provide instruction to patrons and provide them with regular updates about your online reference services. Provide them with short engaging stories they can use during their sessions to explain the value of the services.

- Ensure that your library's reference services are featured prominently in your library's annual reports and signature publications. Establish a strong relationship with your library's administrators to ensure they see and share the impact of the reference services.
- Partner with the information technology experts in your library and in the wider community. As they develop new applications (e.g., a mobile site for the city, library, or university), make sure that your library's reference services are featured prominently.

CHAPTER FIVE

Instruction for Online Patrons

Natalie Haber

Introduction

The American Library Association's *Standards for Distance Learning Library Services* (2016) lists "instruction" as a main library requirement, stating, "The library must provide information and digital literacy instruction programs to the distance learning community." This instruction requirement can be met in a number of different ways. This chapter defines the language surrounding online library instruction and gives ideas and best practices for delivering content. It also provides a brief overview of common technological considerations that should be weighed as you make decisions about purchases and content design.

Studies have found that online library instruction can be just as effective as face-to-face instruction. A study of citations showed "virtually no differences between the performance of the online students versus the face-to-face students" (Clark & Chinburg, 2010, p. 538). Across college campuses, more courses are being moved into the online environment. Technology is becoming easier to use and more supportive of online learning. We have advanced to the point where just about any library instruction can be designed in a meaningful way in the online environment, whether you are teaching a one-shot, a credit-bearing information literacy course, or designing a point-of-need suite of tutorials.

Instructional Design

Online instruction, like any library instruction, benefits from the tenets of instructional design (ID). ID refers to the intentional and systematic process of designing educational materials and lesson plans with the intention of improving student learning and retention of content (Seel, Lehmann, Blumschein, & Podolskiy, 2017). Formal lesson planning is an important piece of online library instruction. There are many strategies for ID; it is in fact a full segment of study within the field of education and cognitive science. This section will help you better understand ID principles and models. To negate the risk of oversimplifying the subject, further reading on this topic is highly recommended.

Learning Outcomes and Backward Design

ID methods are rooted in student learning outcomes. When you start with what students should be able to do by the end of the lesson, it can clarify what content you need to include. This strategy is called "backward design" (Wiggins & McTighe, 2005). Backward design is a three-step process: identifying learning outcomes, determining acceptable assessment, and planning the learning activities.

Learning outcomes should be assessable. This means that they are framed in a way that can be measured. Bloom's Taxonomy can assist you in finding language for your learning outcomes. See https://cft.vanderbilt.edu/guides-sub-pages/blooms-taxonomy/ for examples.

Once you have chosen the main verb that will be used in your learning outcome, you can build out the rest of the sentence. Figure 5.1 shows an easy formula based on the Gilchrist (2015) learning outcomes formula:

Figure 5.1   Learning outcomes formula.

Example:

The student will be able to correctly identify and describe the different types of articles found in a newspaper in order to be able to find appropriate articles for their research papers.

Using learning outcomes to guide your instruction is especially helpful in the online environment. Keeping concrete goals in mind helps you create learning objects that are task-specific and succinct.

ADDIE

The foundational framework for almost all ID models is ADDIE: Analyze, Design, Develop, Implement, and Evaluate. This is a flexible framework that

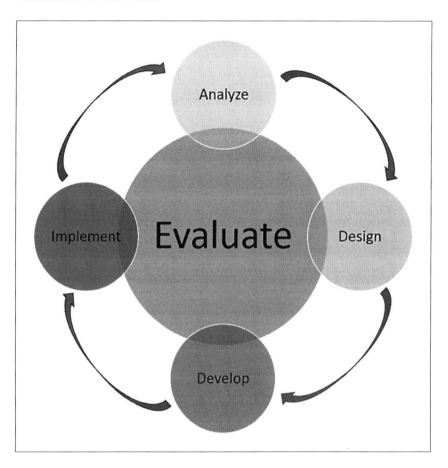

Figure 5.2 The ADDIE concept.

allows for adaptation and revision and focuses on constructing performance-based learning. Figure 5.2 is a graphic representation of the process.

Using an ID model like ADDIE can be especially helpful for new library instructors and can be particularly useful in the online teaching environment.

Example scenario for implementing ADDIE:

A professor has requested online instruction for their HIST 1120 Online course. ADDIE comes into play almost immediately, even as you work with the instructor to decide what the library instruction will look like in the online class.

Analyze: This analysis should start by reaching out to the instructor to find out exactly what their expectations are for the session.

- Has the instructor discussed the upcoming research assignment with students?

- What does the instructor want the students to take away from the online library instruction?
- When does the instructor want the instruction to occur? Timing is important when designing online content. Creating learning objects from scratch takes time and effort.
- What level are the students' research skills before the library instruction? If you're not sure, consider giving a pre-class assessment survey. Include questions about past research experience and what they might hope to learn.

Design: During the design phase, work on creating assessable and achievable learning outcomes for the session. Use pre-class assessments and conversations with the instructor to inform your design. Design is also the time to map out the flow of your plan. For this HIST 1120 Online class, for example, you might plan to include a short introduction, a module that explains newspaper credibility, a demo of the library's resources, and an evaluation. The design is your road map for developing content.

Develop: Once the design is set and approved by the instructor, you can begin to develop the content. Your module that reviews newspaper credibility might be a well-made interactive tutorial, and your demo might be a screencast video of a particular database.

Implement: Implementation is when the content is delivered to the students. Be sure to test your content before it's live. Make sure that your links are accurate and work across all browsers. Test features for students to submit work and get responses.

Evaluate: As you can see from Figure 5.2, evaluation happens throughout this entire process. Evaluate your analysis, design, development, and implementation, and make iterative changes to your approach throughout. Usability testing is one way you can gauge effectiveness throughout the process. At the end, include an assessment that evaluates student learning. In the case of the HIST 1120 class, you could assign a quiz that has them discuss newspaper credibility and describe the process for finding the library's online newspaper collections.

Case Study: Developing Synchronous Library Instruction for Online Nursing Courses

Amanda Calabrese, MSLIS, Online Instruction and Electronic Resources Librarian, *SUNY College of Technology at Delhi, Resnick Library*

SUNY Delhi, located in Delhi, New York is a college of technology in the State University of New York system, offering degrees both on campus and online. Resnick Library serves a student population of approximately 2,700 full-time equivalent enrollment in programs such as nursing, business and hospitality, and veterinary science. The library has strong instructional partnerships with faculty in the School of Nursing, which offers fully online Bachelor of Science in Nursing (BSN) and Master of Science in Nursing (MSN) programs.

In 2014, Resnick Library turned its attention to improving instruction services for online nursing courses. These students were not receiving library instruction comparable to what was available for on-campus programs. This case describes the synchronous library instruction that is now offered for two courses: UNIV 300, Orientation to Online BSN, and NURS 600, Development of the Nurse Educator.

Gaining Instructor Buy-In

As library liaison for nursing, I had previously worked with faculty to update the library content in UNIV 300, an orientation course taken as a prerequisite for BSN coursework. I met with the course coordinator to assess satisfaction with the library video tutorials for the course, and she expressed interest in adding some optional synchronous instruction sessions.

Near the time of this meeting, I provided a workshop to online faculty in the School of Nursing to discuss available library services. I highlighted synchronous library instruction and asynchronous supports such as LibGuides and video tutorials. Many online faculty had previously assumed that instruction was available only for on-campus courses and were interested in exploring synchronous sessions as a way to increase students' use of scholarly resources.

As a result of this workshop, an instructor in the graduate program contacted me about integrating some library content into a new course, NURS 600. This instructor wanted to develop students' skills for writing literature reviews. We collaboratively designed a two-part assignment that required students to first locate and annotate relevant articles and then write a literature review. Students would attend synchronous library instruction one week before annotations were due.

Session Logistics

All sessions are delivered via Zoom, the web meeting platform SUNY Delhi provides. Because the BSN and MSN programs are mostly asynchronous, it is challenging to identify session times convenient for all students. To accommodate their varied schedules, sessions are offered at several different times of day. In UNIV 300, sessions are offered during the week when the existing library content appears in the course, and attendance is optional. In the graduate course, sessions are required, but smaller enrollment makes it easier to identify mutually convenient times.

When sessions for UNIV 300 were first offered, attendance was unsurprisingly poor. Introducing an online sign-up form has improved attendance significantly, with 20–30 students attending each term. Attendance is still optional, but the online sign-up creates accountability for students, and allows me to cancel a session if no one signs up.

Session Content and Response

The content for UNIV 300 highlights the essentials from the video tutorials in the course materials, emphasizing four key skills for locating articles and contacting the library for assistance. I spend most of the session screen-sharing and answering questions from students. In the online format, it is important to balance engaging learning strategies with students' technological comfort level. The BSN program serves many nontraditional students, and in this introductory course, they are often overwhelmed by the technology needed for online coursework. These sessions address very basic web meeting skills such as muting and unmuting their microphones and using the chat feature to communicate.

Students complete an anonymous online evaluation form after each session, and feedback is overwhelmingly positive. Many students comment that seeing a librarian search in real time and having the opportunity to ask questions is extremely valuable, even when they have also watched the video tutorials. Students also appreciate seeing their classmates, since a live web meeting is very different from interacting in text-based discussion forums.

For NURS 600, faculty requested that I teach something more advanced. Students bring one scholarly article to the session, where they are shown how to use the subject headings assigned to that article to locate related sources. They are also taught to use their article's references and metrics to locate referenced/referencing sources. In their annotation assignment, students describe the search strategy used to locate each article and must use the techniques shown in class for at least two articles. I grade this portion of the assignment and, on average, 88 percent of students meet or exceed this requirement.

These sessions incorporate more active learning than is possible in the UNIV 300 sessions. The lesson plan uses polling and an exercise where students share their screens to show their classmates how to apply one of these search techniques.

In follow-up meetings at the end of each semester, course faculty report satisfaction with students' completed literature reviews. Feedback from students is also positive, with many wishing that they had had library instruction earlier in their academic careers. Their input and the success of these two courses provide a solid rationale for seeking additional opportunities to offer synchronous library instruction for online courses.

Bottom Line: Students and faculty in online, asynchronous nursing programs respond positively to synchronous library instruction opportunities when appropriately matched to course level and content.

Doing Good Assessment

All ID models incorporate assessment or evaluation. Assessment can give you a sense of how much your students know going into library instruction, how much your students are learning, how effective your learning objects are, how long your students retain knowledge, or can simply evaluate students in order to give them a grade. Assessment is essential, to inform yourself as an instructor so that you can make changes to improve your teaching, and so that you can report to stakeholders about the effectiveness of online library instruction. In library instruction literature, emphasis is put on classroom assessment, but the same principles should be applied to online learning.

It is particularly important to think of your assessment as a cycle that doesn't end. Megan Oakleaf (2009) advocates assessment to encourage continuous improvement of instruction, which ensures increased student learning. Oakleaf stresses that assessment isn't just about gathering data; it's about using the data to make meaningful changes in your content or approach.

Example:

Enact learning activities: Students were required to complete a worksheet after working through all parts of the library module that you had created. The worksheet had them find two sources. They had to list out the citation information (i.e., title, author, source, date), explain why they believe the source is credible, and justify their choice.

Gather and interpret data: All students were able to find two sources and filled out the worksheet adequately, but as you graded, you realized that many students had not given substantial reasons for why the source is credible. Some students (less than half) had used some language that was included in the module, but most had not.

Make decisions and enact change: It's clear that the portion of the library instruction module that dealt with credibility was not effective. That would be the portion to change. You could try changing the order of the module so that the credibility portion comes first, or perhaps work the content so that it's more engaging by adding more graphics or making it more interactive. Roll those changes out in the next iteration of the course.

It is also worth noting that while it may be tempting, you can't assess everything that you do; you can gather data, but it takes time to analyze data and make changes based on data. Instead of just gathering data without a purpose, it is useful to do some assessment visioning. Look to Mary O'Kelly's *Seven Questions for Assessment Planning* (2015):

1. Responsibility. Who is taking responsibility *and why?*
2. Questions: what questions do we have about our own program *and why?*
3. Data: What information do we need to answer those questions *and why?*
4. Method: How will we get it *and why?*
5. Results: Who will write the answers *and why?*
6. Communication: Who needs to see the results *and why?*
7. Cycle: What is our timeline for changes *and why?*

O'Kelly here is speaking broadly, about library-wide or program-wide assessment efforts, but the same types of questions should be asked as you design an assessment cycle for online library instruction. What are you trying to assess? What's your timeline for changes? Who needs to know?

Assessment Techniques in the Online Environment

Assessment can be done in a number of different ways. There are lots of data points that are easily available to gather: in LibGuides, you can look at page views over time; in YouTube, you can see your views and view length; in learning management systems you can enable view tracking. Other data, particularly about student learning, can be more difficult to ascertain. The following are several different types of assessment that could be used in the online environment.

Qualitative Assessment

This type of assessment is self-reported from your students or the instructor with whom you are working. Qualitative assessment can be gathered in a number of different ways; you could put together a survey, use focus groups, or just send an e-mail requesting feedback. Qualitative assessment often tries to capture individual or group reactions or feelings about the library instruction session.

Communicating with the instructor and encouraging their honest feedback will help you hone in on necessary improvements. Questions to ask include:

- Was the instructor happy with the content you provided?
- Do they have suggestions for content to fill in any gaps?
- Do they feel like their students are doing better research or have more information literacy skills because of the library session?

Surveying students can give you great information too:

- Have you ever had library instruction before? (pre-class questionnaire)
- What are you hoping to get out of the library instruction modules? (pre-class questionnaire)
- Do you feel like the library instruction materials helped you complete your research assignment?
- What was your favorite/least favorite part?
- What was the most useful information you learned?
- What wasn't covered that you wish had been covered?

Quantitative Assessment

Quantitative assessment refers to the hard data: numbers. Online, quantitative assessment takes many forms:

- Citation analysis with a rubric
- Graded quizzes or worksheets
- Number of video or page views
- Average view length of videos or text content
- Discussion forum posts, grade based on number of posts or responses

Self-Reflection

Self-reflection is a key part of assessment that shouldn't be overlooked. Take the time to write a short reflection about how things went with your online instruction. Be sure to include stumbling blocks or things you would change for next time. This type of assessment helps in the long term. Next semester or next year when you create library instruction content for this class, you can easily refresh yourself on the particulars. Self-reflection may be especially important in the online environment; you won't have facial expressions and other nonverbal feedback like you do in a face-to-face class to gauge student engagement and understanding.

Assessment Planning

All forms of assessment take planning. Be sure to clarify the goals of whatever assessment you design. Make sure that there is always a *why* behind each question, and that there are actionable changes that can come out of what you learn.

Comparing Face-to-Face and Online Assessment

Table 5.1 illustrates some of the differences between face-to-face and online assessment.

Table 5.1 Differences between face-to-face and online assessment.

	What level research have students completed before this class?	**How many students were reached through instruction?**
Face-to-Face	At the beginning of class, the librarian could hand out a survey asking the students what types of research they've done, where their interests lie, and any questions they might have. Adjustments to lesson plans can be made on the spot and the librarian can discuss specific interests to increase a sense of community in the classroom.	In a face-to-face class, this could just mean counting the number of students in a section.
Online	Online, a librarian could distribute a survey that asks students about their research and incorporate the findings into the content prepared for the online library instruction session.	In an online class, you can look at a number of data points: how many students enrolled, how many page or video views your content has, how long the average student watched a video.
Main differences	Any time a survey is created, there is more time and planning involved. In the online class, there really is no quick way to gauge student research levels as described in the face-to-face class. If you want that feedback, you'll need to plan to get the survey to students at least a week before so that students have a chance to take the survey and you have a chance to incorporate changes to your content.	In the online environment, data can often give a more in-depth view of student interaction with content. It's up to you to discern which data is the most meaningful to track.

Finding Lesson Plans and Learning Objects

Why reinvent the wheel? If you're pressed for time or looking for new ideas, there are a few great online repositories of lesson plans worth exploring. In addition, there are several places to go for well-made multimedia learning objects.

Lesson plans:

- ACRL Framework for Information Literacy Sandbox: http://sandbox.acrl.org/
- CORA: Community of Online Research Assignments: https://www.project cora.org/

Multimedia learning objects:

- NLA: New Literacies Alliance: https://www.lib.k-state.edu/nla
- PRIMO: Peer-reviewed Instructional Materials Online Database: http://pri modb.org/

Case Study: A Collaborative Model for Online Instructional Design

Teagan Eastman, MLIS, Online Learning Librarian, *Utah State University, Merrill-Cazier Library*

In order to support the 50 academic departments at Utah State University (USU), 22 faculty librarians at USU's Merrill-Cazier Library serve as subject liaisons (SLs). SLs have several responsibilities, including providing information literacy instruction, supporting faculty research, consulting with students, purchasing content, and maintaining subject-specific collections. As the library's SLs are often assigned multiple academic departments and complete their liaison duties on top of other full-time job responsibilities such as serving as the digital scholarship librarian or e-resources librarian, they are often overwhelmed by their workload. An additional challenge for SLs is the high enrollment in USU Online and USU Regional Campus programs. Supporting students in these programs offers unique challenges, as the instructors are often not on the main USU campus and do not realize the library can be a support mechanism in online environments.

In order to ensure that equitable service is provided to USU's online and regional campus students, I was hired to serve as the university's online learning librarian. My role is to create quality online instruction using emerging technologies and best practices. In order to support SLs providing online instruction to their academic departments, I worked with the library's regional campus & e-learning librarian to adapt an instructional design (ID) workflow created by Dominique Turnbow and Amanda Roth from the University of California San Diego (Roth & Turnbow, 2016).

The purpose established for USU's online ID process was to increase integration with online and regional campus courses. In order to minimize time commitments, the design process utilized my online ID experience and the subject matter expertise of our SLs. To this end we created a design document (Figure 5.3) for SLs to use to request online learning objects for online and regional campus classes. This document requires SLs to identify an online instruction need and determine the delivery methods, learning outcomes, and information literacy skills they would like covered in the learning object. In addition to the design document, we created a webpage (https://library.usu.edu/instruct/) with examples of online learning objects to give SLs and USU Online and Regional Campus instructors an idea of what is possible in online instruction.

To introduce this workflow for online ID, I presented the process at a monthly meeting of the SLs. Each SL was given a blank copy of the design document, along with several examples of completed documents and online learning objects. I demonstrated how to identify both online and regional campus courses offered within a liaison's academic department and digital learning objects. To ensure SLs reached out to online and regional campus courses, I created an assignment in which SLs were asked to identify one online or regional campus course within their department, contact the instructor, and determine if there was a research component to the course and thus a need for library instruction. SLs were given a template e-mail to send to instructors that outlined online library instruction possibilities.

After contacting their instructors and identifying a course, SLs were asked to fill out the design document and then meet with me to discuss the creation process. These meetings allowed me to work with SLs to determine how to effectively meet the information literacy needs of students in the course by translating components of their face-to-face instruction sessions into online formats. The SL would provide instructional content (script for a video, text for a module, etc.), and I would create the online learning object(s), integrate them into our learning management system, and set up assessment protocols.

According to data gathered from library-wide instruction statistics, this workflow has increased our support for online and regional campus courses, especially those that have a research component. It has also resulted in the production of higher-quality online learning objects that are developed around course-specific learning outcomes by individuals with subject and ID expertise. Data derived from assessments of student

Design Document

Name of Course & Instructor:
Subject Librarian:
Digital Learning Object Description
Include a brief description of the module/video/tutorial, including method of delivery and how responses/completion will be captured.

Delivery platform: ☐Canvas ☐LibGuides ☐Video ☐Other _____
Course requirement: ☐Yes ☐No
If yes, what should be captured: ☐quiz score ☐object completion
Projected use: _____

Learning Outcomes
Include learning outcomes associated with the object. Only include outcomes that can be assessed through formative or summative methods.

- *Students will be able to...*

IL skills you would like the learning object to cover:
☐ Lit Reviews   ☐ Citation style _____
☐Information Chaining   ☐Types of resources (primary, secondary)
☐ Source evaluation & Use   ☐ How to use catalog/database
☐ Plagiarism   ☐ Selecting a database
☐Synthesis   ☐ Keyword/search terms selection
☐Other _____

Additional content to be covered, but may not include an activity:
Include necessary content that cannot be assessed.

Evaluation
Include your plan for evaluating the "success" of the object as a way of delivering this information. (Don't feel like you have to come up with this on your own).

Project Timeline
Include a detailed project timeline with tasks and who is responsible for completing them

Preparation Time	**(in hours)**
Design	
Stakeholder meetings (SL to also track individual time spent as well)	

Figure 5.3 USU Libraries online learning design document. Adapted from Turnbow and Roth (2016).

learning and feedback from instructors indicates that the online learning objects have improved students' information literacy skills. In addition, it has reduced the time commitment of SLs and eliminated the anxiety of working with unfamiliar technology and systems to create online learning objects.

Bottom Line: Librarians at USU have found that utilizing a design document for the creation of online learning allows librarians to better support online and regional campus courses by creating high-quality learning objects that improve students' information literacy skills.

Scaffolding Online Library Instruction

Scaffolding library instruction refers to spreading learning over time and teaching skills by building on previous skills that students have learned. Scaffolding library instruction is especially important in online instruction. Often, online or distance learning librarians reuse learning objects and modules in online classes. Having a plan for scaffolded instruction helps to reduce the number of times a student might see the same content, which can make them bored, uninterested, and more likely to miss the new content.

Strategies for Scaffolding

Scaffolding Online Library Instruction throughout the Curriculum

In each department, look at the path a student must take to get to graduation. Identify the key courses: which classes do all students in that program have to take (maximize your reach), and in which classes are students completing research? Once those classes have been identified:

- Determine which library skills should be taught in which course.
- Deliver content with the intention of building on the skills students have learned in previous classes.

Scaffolding cannot be achieved in a vacuum; that is, you'll need the cooperation of the department and all the instructors teaching sections of those key courses. If the program is fully online, all library instruction will be online. If the program isn't fully online, you'll also need to work with face-to-face library instructors to create your scaffold. This type of scaffolding takes time to develop.

Scaffolding Online Library Instruction in a Single Class

If you have an embedded role in the class, it may be easier to deliver content throughout the entire research process. For example, some instructors like to split parts of research into sections throughout a course. In a history course, students may be required to find secondary sources for an initial assignment, then primary sources for another assignment later in the semester.

- During the first step of your scaffolded plan, you might tackle just the goal of familiarizing the students with the services available and showing the basics of finding secondary sources.
- The next step in the scaffolded plan would be later in the semester, and you would jump right into using the primary source collections, skipping over the basics of how to use the library's website and requesting help.

Case Study: Personal Librarians for Online Learners

Amanda Ziegler, MLIS, Online Outreach Librarian
Melissa Gonzalez, MLIS, MA, Head of Reference
University of West Florida

The University of West Florida (UWF) Libraries launched its Personal Librarian program in fall 2013. Following the traditional personal librarian model, we targeted all UWF first-time-in-college students. However, in response to considerable increases in the growth of our online learner population in recent years, we also implemented an Online Personal Librarian service for all students enrolled in online programs. The Personal Librarian model allowed us to do direct outreach to this growing student population. As of spring 2017, 33 percent (4,062 of 12,340) of UWF's total headcount were enrolled only in online courses. Students enrolled in an entirely online program are assigned to their corresponding library subject specialist. This tactic proves especially helpful for upper-level and graduate students with more advanced and discipline-specific research needs.

E-mails sent by the librarians serve as a delivery method for customized and chunked asynchronous instruction, as well as opening up a gateway for further connections with the learner, such as synchronous research consultations and online workshops. The goal is to provide individualized outreach and proactive research assistance to students through a direct connection with a librarian. Students receive an initial introductory communication from their personal librarian at the start of the semester, explaining the program and providing the librarian's contact information. After that, personal librarians e-mail students two to three times per semester, highlighting specific resources and services and providing research tips.

The text and schedule of e-mail communications is coordinated by our online outreach librarian, who composes each e-mail and suggests an appropriate subject line. The e-mails that are sent at the beginning of each semester contain an overview of library resources and services for online learners, and direct students to a research guide designed specifically for those learners. The research guide presents a step-by-step tutorial walking students through the basic research process. It links together five short videos covering formulating a research question, selecting and using keywords, discovering and locating sources, selecting relevant articles, and organizing sources for the writing process.

While we strive to keep the text fairly consistent among librarians to ensure that all students receive the same message and information, the point of the program is to develop a relationship with the students that is individualized and capitalizes on each librarian's subject expertise. In the text of a typical e-mail, the librarians include links to two to three library resources. Each librarian customizes the e-mails sent to the students with discipline-specific information. This may include a link to a research guide created for a discipline or database, a link and a brief explanation of a database, short tips for searching in such a database, or directions on how to search for statistics or other information outside of library databases. For instance, the education librarian might include links to state websites containing education data and scorecards, with a few short tips for searching for school success data. The business librarian, while using the same or similar introductory text in the e-mail, might edit the resources offered to highlight a new business database. The instruction presented through the e-mails is also varied throughout the semester with tips on how to access information and request items provided at the beginning and information on citations and creation of scholarly products provided later.

In addition to the asynchronous, customized instruction presented in the e-mails, all e-mails give students the option of contacting their subject specialist librarian for individualized instruction via a research consultation. This process is facilitated by our use of youcanbook.me, a calendar service that allows students to make their own appointments. Most of the research consultations with online students are conducted via Collaborate Ultra, since it allows for video connection and screen sharing, but we also offer students the option to use Skype, Google Hangouts, or phone (often in conjunction with a join.me session). The personal librarian e-mails also serve as a great way to market synchronous online workshops and to distribute links to the recordings of the workshops for asynchronous access after they have taken place.

Bottom Line: A Personal Librarian program targeted at online learners allows for direct contact with the learners, creates a connection, and allows for scaffolded library instruction timed to match student needs at different parts of the semester.

Some Tips for Designing Content

Graphic Design and Text

Sometimes we need students just to read so that they can learn the concepts. This can be challenging. A common refrain in higher education is "Students just don't read anymore!" There are plenty of theories about why that is—chiefly, that daily repeated scrolling through online content causes us to read more shallowly. In asynchronous online classes, students often have to read even more than students in face-to-face sections since the majority of content is conveyed through text. Students who don't read all of what they are given are likely to do poorly in the course. There are several things that you can do to encourage reading of the text you provide if you are designing it yourself (Vai & Sosulski, 2011):

- Use an easy-to-read typeface.
- For accessibility, use a typeface that can be read by screen readers. Look here for a list: http://webaim.org/techniques/fonts/
- Keep right margins jagged.
- Put ample space between lines of text.
- Keep it uncluttered. White space is good, no crowding.
- Use bold type sparingly and for emphasis.
- Be consistent with all graphic elements.

Chunking

To avoid information overload, practice chunking, which means dividing your content into short modules. Not only will students stay more engaged with the content, but when you create smaller chunks, you can easily reuse and rearrange content for other classes. Being able to reuse content is ideal; it will save time in the long run. Creating smaller chunks of content also allows for an easier refresh. Instead of having to rebuild an entire lengthy tutorial, you can just replace the part that needs updating.

Active Learning and Motivation

Active learning allows students to engage more deeply with content, interact with their peers, and construct their own knowledge. Engagement and motivation go hand in hand. Active learning and student motivation are both essential for quality online courses and can be achieved in a number of different ways. Here are some ideas:

- Passive to active: Whenever you have students watch or read something, follow up by having them complete an exercise that has them practice what they just saw.
- Quizzes and worksheets: Help to keep students engaged until the end of a video or text.
- Discussion boards: Utilize the discussion board to lead a group discussion. This could be formally or loosely structured, graded or not. Ask students to describe their research process in a post or invite students to ask any research questions they have.
- Pair them up: Set up a pair/share activity that has students applying what they have learned from the module as a team. Sharing back could be directly with you or with the whole class in a discussion forum.
- Develop a community: Students are more motivated when they feel that they are a part of something.

  - Consider creating a short introductory video about yourself so that students can put a face with your name, or simply attach an image to your profile.
  - In for-credit classes, do some online icebreakers so that students can get to know one another.

- Peer teaching: Have students create short videos, infographics, or other learning objects in order to teach research concepts to one another.

Case Study: Engaging Students during Synchronous Library Instruction

Michael LaMagna, EdD, Associate Professor & Reference Librarian;
Information Literacy Program and Library Services Coordinator,
Delaware County Community College, Learning Commons

At Delaware County Community College, our information literacy program did not offer online and hybrid learners the same level of instruction received by our traditional on-campus students. In an effort to better serve the educational needs of this growing student population, Library Services initiated a synchronous, non-credit, online workshop model in 2013 as part of the larger information literacy program offered at the institution. In addition to supporting a growing online and hybrid student population, another goal of this online workshop program was to support students at our branch campus locations in Delaware and Chester Counties in southeastern Pennsylvania. Initially, Library Services offered 10 online, synchronous workshops with a total registration of 135 students. Since then, it has grown to approximately 50 workshops each semester. While students are often encouraged to participate in one of these workshops by their professors, the majority of students voluntarily attend. During this period of growth, library faculty focused on ensuring each workshop was engaging and included active learning components. As librarians who have attended synchronous online professional development opportunities, we are well aware of the challenges involved in keeping attendees' attention focused on the content.

We investigated a number of web-conferencing software programs and selected GoToTraining because of its features and functionality. This included the standard participant engagement features such as polling, hand raising, chat, and collaboration through productivity software documents in addition to the ability to determine when students became inattentive (e.g., when students minimize the screen or open additional browsers). To ensure student participation, we begin each session by discussing the features of the web-conference technology to ensure students are able to use the program.

While each faculty librarian has the academic freedom to design their workshop, we have some best practices to ensure an engaging learning environment. Each workshop we offer has an advertised description of what will be covered. We begin each workshop session with a few quick polls to better understand the needs of those in attendance. These include general questions geared to understanding what students hope to learn during the workshop. These ice-breaker poll questions can range from "Have you attended any previous workshops" to "What citation style do you anticipate using as part of your research assignment?" The additional goal of these questions is to set the expectation that the workshop will require participation. Although the workshops are mostly prepared in advance, knowledge of the students' motivations for attending allows us to customize the content to meet the specific needs of the group. After the initial questions, we include a poll question roughly every 15 minutes to keep the students engaged. They are similar to questions that we would ask during a classroom information literacy session. A benefit to using the polling feature is that the results of the polls can be displayed to all attendees so they can compare their responses to those of their peers. Having the ability to identify those students who have become inattentive through the software allows us to draw these students back into the conversation through polls and chat.

Another feature of our web-conferencing software is chat. This is an excellent tool for engaging students by encouraging them to ask questions during the workshop session. It also allows us to provide helpful links and other content. For example, when transitioning from a prepared presentation to a live demonstration, we include the link to the web page being displayed to ensure students are able to follow along with the instructions. Doing this at the start of the workshop teaches students where they can find helpful links during the session and where they can look if they become lost during the workshop. It also ensures they know where the chat function is located so they can ask questions when they arise.

To engage students through active learning, we include activities during the workshop either through material distributed electronically before the workshop, during the workshop through a materials feature in the software, or by linking to a Google Doc. While all options ensure each student has access to the material, the Google Doc allows for real-time collaboration. This could be editing a citation as a group or developing a research question.

Bottom Line: It is important to keep students engaged during synchronous instructional sessions. We have found that features of web-conferencing software can help tremendously. Periodically polling students offers an engaging activity while identifying who may not be attentive. This offers an opportunity for those teaching the workshop to engage the student in the chat. Informal assessment reveals this approach resulting in the growth of our online, synchronous workshop program.

Best Practices for Creating Videos

Screencasts Work

Research shows that students are receptive to screencast-style learning. This format is popular with both librarians and students. Students do well using them—particularly for lower-level learning and reviewing higher-level learning concepts (Martin & Martin, 2014).

Length

Research shows that students prefer screencasts to be short! Create videos that run less than three minutes (Baker, 2014). Viewers rarely watch an entire video. Put the most important information at the beginning of the video.

Speed and Tone of Speech

Narration speed is important. Speak slowly enough so that viewers can keep up, but not so slowly that they lose interest and close the video. Research suggests that an ideal pace is three words per second (Baker, 2014). Avoid a monotone voice, or viewers may lose interest.

Born Accessible

Strive to make all videos accessible to all of your viewers from the moment they are created. To stay in compliance with guidelines from the Americans with Disabilities Act (ADA) all videos must include closed captioning (CC) or a transcript (U.S. Department of Justice, n.d.). YouTube has a free CC tool that is user friendly.

Some Tools to Consider

Choosing which software you are going to invest time and money into is important for online library instruction. This list was generated from an online discussion called "Tools for Online Learning" hosted by the Association of College and Research Libraries' (ACRL's) Distance Learning Section in March 2017.

Screencasting

Screencasting can be great for showing PowerPoint presentations or demonstrating how to use a database or the library's website. Here are some recommended software options:

- Jing: TechSmith's free screen capture and screencast software application. Very little editing can be done to videos, but it's good for a quick screencast. https://www.techsmith.com/jing-tool.html
- Camtasia: User friendly with a mild learning curve. Not cheap, but it has a lot of bells and whistles, and TechSmith has a fair number of tutorials to get you started https://www.techsmith.com/camtasia.html
- Microsoft PowerPoint: Has built-in recording features. Microsoft Office products are likely already installed at your library. https://microsoft-powerpoint-2016.en.softonic.com/

Animated Tutorials

Animation can help make your videos more enjoyable and less dry for your students.

- Powtoons: User-friendly software that allows you to create animated short videos. Great for teaching information literacy concepts. A free version is available. https://www.powtoon.com/
- VideoScribe: Animated whiteboard-style videos. Pricey, but depending on your needs it could be a worthy investment. http://www.videoscribe.co/

Interactive Tutorials

Adding interaction to your tutorials can help students stay focused throughout the entire tutorial.

- Captivate: Pricey and takes some work to learn. Very comprehensive software. Allows you to screencast, add animations, and make tutorials interactive. http://www.adobe.com/products/captivate/education.html
- Guide on the Side: Free. Created and shared by the University of Arizona. May require assistance from IT to set up as it needs SMTP server support. Has a panel along the left side of the screen for the tutorial alongside the live website. https://ualibraries.github.io/Guide-on-the-Side/about.html
- Storyline: Makes it very easy to create interactive tutorials. Mobile-friendly with responsive design. Expensive, robust software. https://www.articulate .com/products/storyline-why.php
- LibWizard—Springshare product. Integrated into a software product with which many librarians are already familiar. Very simple way to create interactive tutorials, quizzes, and surveys. https://www.springshare.com/libwizard/

Case Study: Creating Free Online Branching Games with PowerPoint Skills

Ian Boucher, MLIS, Emerging Technologies and Outreach Librarian, *North Carolina Wesleyan College, Elizabeth Braswell Pearsall Library*

Games provide opportunities for students to actively apply and build their understandings of concepts. This presents great potential for online students, who must engage with course content on their own schedules. At North Carolina Wesleyan College, there are many adult students with busy schedules outside of classes, and not all campuses have libraries. These students' experiences of library resources are almost entirely online. As the emerging technologies and outreach librarian, one of my tasks is to develop tools these students can access and learn from at times appropriate for their schedules. When the college's instructional technologist introduced me to Office Mix, a free screencasting add-on for PowerPoint that allowed content to remain clickable after being posted online, I used it to develop an interactive game for students to play as an engaging, experiential introduction to finding scholarly, peer-reviewed journal articles. This experience has provided me with skills invaluable for my educational endeavors.

"NCWC Library: Journal Quest" is the first in what I hope to be a series of games that will help students and faculty navigate important library concepts. It can be used independently or as a supplement to instruction, whenever students may need it. My hope is that this game will cultivate my library's ability to vividly introduce more of our students to what we have to offer and strengthen our face-to-face instruction. If students complete the game before live instruction sessions, instructors can use class time to deepen understandings of library research.

Students log in with their college credentials, activate the "Click to Play" button, and are presented with four characters, each based on a popular major at the college: Sam Sports, Betty Business, C.J. (short for Criminal Justice), and Caroline Computers. Players must navigate through a scenario, helping their characters find a scholarly, peer-reviewed journal article. Players locate library databases, select the best database for the task, use filters to narrow the search, and analyze three abstracts to choose the best article. More than a guided demonstration, players must explore several relevant situations and exercise critical decisions to find their way to the next point. If a player selects an incorrect answer, the game provides encouraging feedback elaborating on why the answer was wrong before returning to the previous screen. At the end of the game, there is a brief quiz on the concepts, as well as questions for feedback. The game relies on a basic story premise, clip art, and clear fonts and contrasts to communicate clearly with as many players as possible.

"NCWC Library: Journal Quest" is essentially a PowerPoint presentation disguised as a game and posted online, with players clicking on buttons that take them to specified slides. All I needed to build it was PowerPoint, as well as public domain images. No animations were needed. By right-clicking on pictures, text boxes, or other objects I wanted to turn into buttons, and hyperlinking them to other slides within the presentation, I was able to lead players to any slides I wished, allowing players to make decisions affecting their progress in the game. In fact, if players were to click through each slide as a presentation without clicking on the buttons, they would get lost very quickly! To ensure that students do not accidentally click on empty space and go to the wrong slide, a colleague recommended that I place a giant, invisible text box in front of all unnecessary content on each slide. I designed the quiz at the end using Office Mix's built-in quiz apps, and required students to log in so that their answers could be retrieved by name from the library's free Office Mix account and individually assessed by faculty.

Like many projects, this will continue to be a process of experimentation. It began as an underwater adventure game in which students needed to assemble a treasure chest, follow a sea turtle, and use library resources to outsmart a giant octopus. I honed it through collaboration with students, faculty, and staff to find the best fit for our community's needs, working with branch campus directors and instructors to test the game in courses. Technology, however, is tenuous. A few months after the game went live, Office Mix announced it would be retiring. Fortunately, relevant skills continue to develop alongside and across platforms, and the most important takeaway of this case is that these skills can be applied anywhere in which slides can be linked to one another and to online forms. For instance, a similar gaming experience can be created using Google Slides and Google Forms, where I plan to adapt "NCWC Library: Journal Quest" and build future games. Linking presentation slides to create interactive online games presents an invaluable, vast, branching array of possibilities for providing students with the support, guidance, and foundation to create their own stories.

Bottom Line: Using basic PowerPoint skills, you can create free online games to provide applied, asynchronous, and engaging library instruction experiences.

Technological Considerations

Choosing software should be approached thoughtfully. For many institutions, software requests require a formal proposal and aren't made frequently. The software that a distance or online learning librarian has available can greatly impact the quality and interactivity of the materials created. Whenever you are making technology-purchasing decisions or choosing to invest time into learning new software, consider the following:

- **Software expense**
  - How much does it cost?
  - Do you have the financial support to make this purchase?
  - Is this a one-time purchase or an ongoing subscription?
- **Licensing**
  - Do you want this software installed on one computer, several, or library-wide?

- Does the software company offer special educational pricing? What does that process look like?
- Will students be using it? If so, can it be used by off-campus students?
- Does someone else on campus already have a license for it?

- **Learning Curve**

  - How much time does it take to learn?
  - Does the software company provide tutorials to help you learn how to use it?
  - How much time can you or your staff dedicate to learning it?

- **Accessibility**

  - Does the software meet the ADA standards (U.S. Department of Justice, n.d.)?
  - Does the software create content that is responsive for mobile viewing?

- **Compatibility**

  - Is the software platform agnostic, or does it require a specific operating system?
  - Does the content work across major browsers?

- **Version upgrades**

  - How often is this software upgraded?
  - What does it cost to upgrade, or are new versions available for free?

- **Support**

  - What type of support does the company offer?
  - Can your organization offer support?

- **Analytics**

  - Does the company provide analytics or usage statistics?

Conclusion

Providing instruction for online library patrons is essential. With an increased emphasis on online learning at nearly every institution of higher education, it's important for librarians to stay ahead of the curve. Online library instruction should incorporate the tenets of ID and formal assessment plans. Whether you are teaching a one-shot online class, taking on an embedded role in a course throughout the semester, teaching a for-credit course, or making your library's web page more pedagogical in nature, using the ideas and best practices found in this chapter will be beneficial.

CHAPTER SIX

Embedded Librarianship

Elaine Sullo

Introduction

Librarians traditionally provide assistance to students, staff, faculty, and researchers in the library, and more recently outside of the library by visiting academic departments or holding off-site library office hours. The embedded role itself is evolving; the first embedded librarians, in their "away-from-the-library" physical spaces, paved the way for the next generation of embedded librarians. They are not only serving patrons in locations outside of the library but are also joining online classrooms, research teams, and curriculum developers in providing personal, customized, high-quality service.

What Is Embedded Librarianship?

Embedded librarianship has been described in a variety of ways by many librarian authors. Here is a sample of how embedded librarianship has been defined:

- . . . it involves focusing on the needs of one or more specific groups, building relationships with these groups, developing a deep understanding of their work, and providing information services that are highly customized and targeted to their greatest needs. (Shumaker & Talley, 2009, p. 9)
- . . . a new paradigm of librarianship to take library services and resources to the user, regardless of the user's locale, through various effective routes that will meet the needs of users. (Lemley, 2016, p. 232)
- . . . takes a librarian out of the context of the traditional library and places him or her in an "on site" setting or situation that enables close coordination and collaboration with researchers or teaching faculty. (Carlson & Kneale, 2011, p. 167)

As these definitions suggest, embedded librarianship involves providing information services to users, whether they are in a classroom a short distance from the library or halfway around the world. Contrary to traditional librarianship where librarians provide assistance when asked or approached, embedded librarians place themselves in the space (physical or virtual) of their patrons, and become a collaborative partner while proactively anticipating users' needs.

Models of Embedded Librarianship

For online patrons, the most common model of embedded librarianship involves virtually embedded librarians. These librarians provide service to online education students and faculty by delivering customized information services for a particular course via the institution's learning management system (LMS). This model is a partnership between the librarian and the instructor who is teaching the course, as both parties are invested in the academic success of the students. As an instructional collaborator, you will decide with the instructor the level of your embeddedness or involvement as well as the time period. You can be embedded in the online course for an entire semester or for a defined period of time that coincides with students' research-based assignments. Once an agreement has been made, the instructor gives you access to the online class by adding you as a co-instructor or a teaching assistant. Some institutions have created a librarian role in the institution's LMS for this purpose. With these arrangements, you will have access to all aspects of the course, including the syllabus, course content, weekly assignments, discussion board posts, and other class resources. Some of the possible responsibilities of a virtual embedded librarian are listed here:

- Contribute/create course content
- Provide feedback on student assignments
- Deliver online instruction (both synchronous and asynchronous)
- Provide links to tutorials or research guides
- Answer student questions via the "Ask the Librarian" discussion board
- Support student research, such as citing sources and choosing appropriate databases
- Provide links to library resources (e.g., for assigned readings)
- Assist students, faculty, and researchers with finding the full text of articles, and provide help using interlibrary loan if full text is not available
- Offer online office hours
- Provide reference service through e-mail, telephone, or an online meeting platform
- Provide assistance with literature searches for students/perform literature searches for faculty and researchers

- Offer online or in-person consultations (not all distance education students are actually at a distance)
- Troubleshoot technology issues
- Assist faculty with online library access

Outside of the LMS, you may work closely online with research teams, project management teams, or faculty engaged in specific curricular initiatives. In these experiences, instead of students, the patrons are researchers, administrators, clinicians, and other professionals. While the population may be different, the roles and responsibilities of the embedded librarian are the same: build collaborative relationships with fellow team members, deeply understand the focus of their work, anticipate their information needs, and take shared responsibility for project outcomes (Shumaker & Talley, 2009). For example, you might be part of a research team comprising faculty from several institutions who are conducting a systematic review. Each member of the team has specific responsibilities; your role might include suggesting relevant databases, creating a list of keywords and subject headings, creating the search strategy and conducting the search, documenting and managing search results, obtaining the items, and perhaps writing the methods section for the publication.

Time Commitment

As with most academic endeavors, the amount of time spent being an embedded librarian depends on many factors. Of course, time commitment varies depending on the number of course sections assigned and the number of students in each section. Within the LMS, the time commitment varies according to course responsibilities and level of embeddedness. For example, if you are only monitoring the "Ask the Librarian" discussion board, the time commitment will be much less than if you are also providing feedback on students' literature searching assignments and reference list format. Student demographics/characteristics may also affect the amount of time that you spend in the classroom. Technology expertise and prior use of online databases and research tools play into the classroom dynamics and into the amount and level of assistance or guidance needed. In addition, you may be active in the classroom throughout the entire semester, or you may be needed only during specific weeks where an assignment or a discussion board is directly related to your areas of expertise. Likewise, if you are asked to create video welcome messages, online tutorials, or information literacy research guides, you will certainly spend additional time on these tasks.

Another consideration related to time is your hours of availability and turnaround time for providing feedback or answers to discussion board questions or e-mailed questions. Some librarians may strictly provide service during the traditional workday, while others plan to be available in the evenings or on weekends. Many of these factors related to time commitment also apply to work with online researchers. If you are involved in a project with a short timeline, such as a grant proposal, they may have different expectations of you than another researcher working on a systematic review. In addition, there may be frequent conference calls or online meetings based on team progress and upcoming deadlines.

Aside from the embedded librarian classroom responsibilities, take into account whether there is specific training needed for this new role, and if so, consider the time commitment required. Librarians who are newly embedded into an institution's LMS may not have the necessary experience to swiftly navigate the online classroom. In addition, if you are planning to teach or hold online office hours, you may need to become familiar with collaborative tools within, and outside of, the LMS. If you are embedded in an online research team, you may need to take time to learn about the area being studied, as well as the terminology used in the discipline.

Several staffing questions affect both time commitment and the day-to-day operations of library departments:

- Will all reference/information services librarians have embedded responsibilities, or will only certain librarians do this work?
- Will the workload be evenly divided among librarians, or will those with liaison duties or subject expertise participate more extensively in the embedded role?
- How will time spent being an embedded librarian impact other responsibilities?
- How will the library handle online classroom duties and teaching when the embedded librarian is away from the office?

The Practicalities of Providing Embedded Librarian Services

As knowledge of the service spreads and the requests for virtual embedded librarians in the online classroom increase, several best practices can help to keep librarians, faculty, and administrators on track.

First, coordinate embedded librarian requests before each semester begins. It is helpful to appoint one person (either a faculty member in the group served or a librarian), to put a call out for embedded librarian requests in that population (e.g., in the School of Nursing), and indicate a date by which requests must be received. The following is an e-mail template that could be sent to faculty:

Dear nursing faculty,

The fall semester is almost upon us! As in previous semesters, librarians are available to be embedded in your online courses. An embedded librarian can:

– Answer student questions in an "Ask the Librarian" discussion board
– Assist students in using APA citation format
– Assist with literature searches and provide research support
– Assist in using library resources (databases, RefWorks, eBooks, etc.)
– Conduct online training sessions

If you would like to request an embedded librarian for your fall semester course, please e-mail me by August 20 with the following information:

• Course number and title
• Number of sections (if there are multiple sections)
• Time frame (is the embedded librarian needed for the entire semester or only during specific weeks?)

Please feel free to contact me with questions as well.

Thank you,
Elaine

Once requests have been submitted, assign librarians to courses, keeping in mind their workload and other responsibilities. If there are multiple sections of the same course with different assigned librarians, differences in librarian practices may need to be discussed. Contact the instructors for the assigned classes to discuss expectations and responsibilities.

Second, recognize that students may be hesitant to reach out to you at first, and an engaging, approachable tone can go a long way. This can include the following:

• With the instructor's permission, add your photograph and contact information to the instructor information in the classroom.
• Ask the instructor to introduce and endorse you in an e-mail or announcement to students.
• At the beginning of the semester (or time period), send a welcome e-mail to students. Communicate availability and types of assistance you can provide, and invite students to contact you.
• Set up an "Ask the Librarian" discussion board and encourage students to post questions.

- During the semester, or as the class winds down, let the students know that you are still accessible and available to provide individual assistance, even after the class is over.

If you work with faculty or researchers, or if you may have future opportunities to work in this capacity, engagement might include:

- Sending a welcome e-mail or postcard to new faculty members
- Offering to introduce yourself via an online meeting and promote the knowledge and skills that may be relevant to that faculty member's interests or area of study

Lastly, keep statistics regarding the number of embedded librarians, the number of classes, the number of sections, the number of students, and the number of research projects. Document feedback provided by students and faculty on the experience. This data can be used for future marketing and promotion of the embedded librarian service.

Case Study: A Model of Integrated Learning

Reed Garber-Pearson, MLIS, Integrated Social Sciences & Online Learning Librarian, *University of Washington Libraries*

I am the librarian for an online degree completion program at the University of Washington. While my home and promotional process is within the University Libraries, I am a core staff member of the program I serve, Integrated Social Sciences (ISS). The position is a new model for the Libraries, expanding the traditional purview of liaison work. I am funded directly through ISS, and I dedicate the bulk of my time to outreach and curriculum/course development. My day-to-day activities include co-teaching with faculty, building course content and learning objects, participating in curriculum revisions, and providing direct student learning support. I am currently exploring solutions to some challenges in online student engagement and digital pedagogy by using a model of curriculum integration and targeted programming.

ISS students are required to take five core classes that provide a foundational understanding of interdisciplinary social science theory and research methodology. Cumulative electronic portfolios showcase academic papers, sets of social science keyword definitions, and reflections that integrate academic learning into community impacts and needs. Early in the research process students learn to identify a clear audience and stakeholders in their inquiry, write op-ed letters, and identify popular information that is based on academic research.

The program has recently undergone a complete curriculum revision. Over the course of three retreat days, ISS faculty, academic advisers, and I overhauled the syllabus of each core course, constructed new learning goals, and divided content revisions. As a result, I have created material for each course: scaffolding elements of web, media, and information literacy to align with broader learning goals and assignments. This deviates from previous course models that have relied on one modular week to present information literacy and library skills. For example, in the second week of their first course students are introduced to our basic library resources and discuss confirmation bias in inquiry. This is directly tied to the week's assignment of learning to read an academic article. By the end of their final course, students have moved through posing questions and refining topics, search strategies on the free web and in article databases, gathering background information, source evaluation, and lateral reading skills, identifying multiple voices and perspectives, and citation formatting. The major skills that students learn are intentionally placed to prepare them to find a variety of materials, narrow and expand inquiries, and evaluate information intake in various contexts. To support this curriculum integration, I e-mail bi-weekly research tips and suggestions to the program's student listserv, aligning resources with that week's current skills and topics of study. Sending these tailored tips and resources would not be possible without my full integration and knowledge of student assignments and depth of questions.

The online learning environment can feel very calculated for students and instructors alike. When I began supporting an asynchronous online program, I found student connection limited—between students themselves, and between myself and students. I was creating learning objects without having any contact directly with students. I have relied on student surveys to give me feedback. With the growing dependency on learning management systems (LMS) to organize content and create opportunities for engagement, connection and pedagogy has become more constrained. While our LMS easily organizes content, it can also prescribe a rigid and unrealistic workflow, limiting pedagogical approaches. For example, Canvas uses modules to group and display learning concepts and time periods within a course. Students flip through modules by using a "next" button, prescribing a linear learning process. Dialogue occurs in weekly discussion boards with students often restricting themselves to the mandatory two posts. Having the flexibility and freedom to collaborate with faculty, build new assignments and learning objects, and review the entirety of the curriculum has enabled me to think differently about these routine approaches to online pedagogy and engagement. Course analytics reveal that students do not watch all videos or necessarily move through modules linearly, instead preferring to jump through concepts and materials more freely. As a consequence, we are slowly eliminating long video lectures and quizzes and replacing them with chunked content, smaller concepts, and activities that are grouped accordingly. Longer interviews with faculty and video presentations are moving to a YouTube channel where students can access this content at-need, though viewing is not required.

To encourage student interaction beyond the discussion boards, I have piloted online study hours and research "happy hours," but they have been poorly attended. In response to a survey about extracurricular programs, I am currently launching a new workshop program for ISS students called digital storytelling. This program has been previously piloted at the UW Libraries, but as a fellowship for select graduate students. This iteration guides students in building narration around using academic knowledge outside the classroom, and a creating a digital product that is incorporated directly into portfolios. Using WeVideo, a cloud-based video editing program, students participate in asynchronous workshopping with virtual drop-in hours for hands-on support. A Slack channel gives an opportunity for more dynamic conversation to occur. The process prepares students to be digital content creators and to translate academic knowledge into a popular context. While this Libraries-offered program is still in pilot mode, digital storytelling is being considered for integration into the capstone course and is an exciting model for online learning outside the LMS.

Bottom Line: Library skills and resources best engage students in online programs when intentionally scaffolded and integrated into the entirety of the curriculum and academic workflow. Digital storytelling workshops are being piloted as a way to engage students outside of the LMS space.

Impact on Student Learning

Ultimately, assessing whether students' information literacy and research skills have improved will help to evaluate the success of an embedded librarian within an online course. Evaluation methods include the following:

- Administer an information literacy skills quiz at the beginning of the semester and then at the end of the semester after the embedded librarian experience. Alternatively, students could reflect upon their experiences and conduct a self-assessment of information literacy skills.
- Conduct citation analysis of student research papers. Citation analysis can be qualitative or quantitative and can be used to evaluate the number and quality

of resources cited in student reference lists. Instructors and librarians can examine the types of resources used, as well as their overall quality and appropriateness for the topic.

• Ask for feedback from those involved (faculty, instructors, students) regarding the experience of interacting with the embedded librarian and whether this experience impacted student learning and quality of scholarly work.

• Measure the impact of word of mouth; has there been a growing demand from faculty for embedded librarian services? Embedded librarian initiatives often start with a pilot program or with only a few librarians and online courses. As word spreads among faculty, the number of requests for an embedded librarian will increase.

• Gather other data that may be indicative of the success of the faculty/librarian classroom collaboration. Evaluate the number and type of reference questions asked, the number of student consultations conducted, and the number of online instruction sessions with the number of attendees.

Conclusion

Customized services, a deep understanding of the subject domain, relationships built on shared goals, and interactions with patrons outside of the four walls of the library are at the core of embedded librarianship. In the online classroom, the collaboration between librarian and faculty member provides a diverse learning experience for students, with knowledge and expertise from different perspectives that can contribute to students' learning and information literacy skills. You have the opportunity, in working with students, instructors, and researchers, to bring your skills and experience directly to the patron at the exact time that they are needed and valued.

CHAPTER SEVEN

Relationship Building

Karla Aleman

Introduction

Building connections to online library patrons requires library staff to reach out to those individuals directly and to develop relationships with different people and groups with whom these patrons interact. Fostering relationships, collaborations, and partnerships creates opportunities for library staff to meet online patrons where they are—in the environments where they learn, seek information, and explore their own voices—even when those places are not the physical library. With greater connection and integration into patrons' lives, library services and resources become more convenient, more accessible, and therefore more relevant to patrons as they navigate today's information-rich world. The challenge for libraries comes in the diversity of potential associates and partners, the many different types of relationships possible, and the unique organizational structures of individual libraries and their institutions, all of which make relationship building a complicated, but exciting, endeavor that requires some thought and planning to execute well. This chapter covers the various options and methods for developing relationships, collaborations, and partnerships that help connect the library to online patrons and improve the quality of the connection.

Reasons for Building Relationships

Relationships have the potential to bring disparate talents and perspectives together to accomplish a variety of goals, but knowing where to start can be a challenge. With many libraries and institutions working with limited resources, deciding where to focus often leads to discoveries of intersections between where they can make the most impact in the lives of their patrons and where the most support is available. The following steps will guide you through these decisions.

Mission, Vision, and Goals

Building from Chapter 1, "Taking Stock of Your Library," start with the library's mission, vision, and goals. Analyze the library's core strategic plan (if there is one) to see where online patrons fit. For those libraries without a strategic plan, consider reviewing informal planning documents (e.g., meeting minutes and budget allocations) and discussing the library's goals with library leadership. Next review the institution's strategic plan, priorities, and goals. When reviewing these documents, ask the following questions:

About the library strategic plan:

- Does the strategic plan include specific goals related to online learning and library resources?
- Are there library-wide goals for increasing online resources or acquiring new online formats (e.g., streaming video)?
- Are there goals for improving research instruction?
- What are the goals related to the library's website?

About the institutional strategic plan:

- Does the institution plan to increase the number of online courses and programs offered?
- Is there a campus-wide movement toward open educational resources?
- Is there an initiative to improve accessibility of electronic resources across campus?
- Are dual enrollment programs at local high schools getting special attention?
- What campus initiatives for online education would benefit from library participation?

Also, review the strategic plans of external organizations, including local school districts, public libraries, and others, to see where your library can help. Use your list of strategic priorities and goals related to online patrons and services to identify the individuals and groups responsible for accomplishing these goals. These potential partners may have additional resources (e.g., funding and staff support), and their work may align with your priorities in improving the quality of the service to online patrons.

User Experience

In order to flesh out your priorities, evaluate the current user experience for online students using the library. The U.S. Department of Health and Human Services (HHS) provides standards for user experience design at https://web-standards.hhs.gov/guidelines/. Scan the library's digital environments, from its website and research guides to its catalog and databases through the lens of user experience, using the standards as a guide. Are there areas where the user experience can be improved? With this initial scan, you may identify the more obvious areas in the library's digital environments where improvements are needed. Review the data you have access to, from usage statistics to error reports. If time and resources allow, conduct simple usability tests with your patrons. HHS's overview of usability testing and resources for testing can be found at https://www.usability.gov/.

Seeing where improvements are needed can be an easy way to create a list of changes, many of which may require collaborating with various library departments or outside partners to accomplish. Are there places where fixing the problem areas would facilitate the strategic initiatives? In comparing the lists of strategic goals and potential user experience improvements, you may find overlap, allowing you to prioritize your own goals around both broader strategic initiatives and the specific needs of your online patrons.

Connecting with Partners

Possible Associates

Libraries, institutions, and communities are filled with possible associates, collaborators, and partners. Whether it is a connection made at a local library conference or a question asked by a faculty member at a committee meeting, the connections individual library employees make with other people in the library, at the institution, and outside of the institution may turn into full-fledged collaborations and partnerships.

Inside the Library

Specific library staff. Some goals require working with individual library staff, particularly those who perform targeted, discipline-specific outreach and those with a technology emphasis. Possible associates include:

- Subject or liaison librarians
- Web librarian

- System librarian or administrator
- Library outreach coordinator

Services and collections. Some goals require working with entire departments or units, particularly those currently working in or moving into the digital environment. Possible associates include:

- Instruction and reference department(s)
- Circulation and course reserves
- Interlibrary loan
- Archives and the digital repository
- Marketing and communications

Inside the Institution

Students. Students (distance and online students in particular) are a key resource for insight into the student experience. Student partners bring not only this perspective but also their emerging technical skills in instruction, marketing, and programming. Partnerships with students and student groups may mean a combination of soliciting their input throughout the strategic planning process and working with them in creating and managing new or improved library programs. You can also work with students to be representatives for the library when peer-to-peer relationships are necessary, for example, in conducting focus groups or offering peer mentoring (Johnson, Clapp, Ewing, & Buhler, 2011). Possible associates include:

- Student government (particularly the distance/online student representatives)
- Student life office
- Current and alumni distance student groups and e-mail distribution lists
- Online student ambassadors
- Students in related academic programs such as education technology or library science

Faculty and instructors. As the primary contact for most students, instructors have the potential to greatly increase the library's connection to, and importance for, the students in their courses. By including activities such as research assignments that require library resources or discussion forums where librarians monitor the responses and provide feedback, instructors can build library–student engagement into their courses. Specific people to reach out to include:

- Online instructors
- Academic program coordinators
- Dual-enrollment coordinators and high school teachers

Case Study: A Train-the-Trainer Course
for Faculty Instructors

Shauna Edson, MLIS, Instructional Design Librarian, *University of Wisconsin-Parkside Library*

This case study describes the development of a train-the-trainer course designed for faculty instructors at the Distance Education Summer Workshop (referred to as Workshop) at the University of Wisconsin-Parkside. My goal was to introduce faculty instructors to library learning objectives, get them to practice using the library tools, and consult with them on where to insert library research in their courses.

I began my project by analyzing participants' competencies, skills, knowledge, and motivations to ensure that I was designing at the appropriate level. The 13 instructors in the Workshop were already expert researchers, though they had varying experience with library resources and services. Their teaching experience was largely limited to in-person instruction, and they had varying levels of mastery of digital tools.

Next, I completed a task analysis to determine what skills and knowledge a participant would need to be successful in the Workshop. This was incredibly illuminating because it reinforced the need for scaffolding to increase participant confidence in their own technical skills. For example, I wanted instructors to familiarize themselves with subject-specific database content on our website so they would feel comfortable using these research tools within their own online courses. The task analysis broke it down even further: go to the library website, find the subject-specific databases, use the database tools, understand database content, link to the database, and embed database content. Breaking these steps down with a task analysis allowed me to slowly build the knowledge and confidence of instructors (Bell, Andrews, & Wulfuk, 2009).

Grouping tasks that seemed to fit together, I began writing objectives to communicate to participants what would be taught and when. One grouping included the following three tasks: gather and organize background information on a topic; use websites, periodicals, and books to gather information on a topic; and cite sources correctly. I combined those tasks and summarized with the following objective: Identify the characteristics of popular sources in the research process. After writing my course objectives, I organized each into four modules, knowing that I would have four in-class instruction opportunities with the participants.

I used Horton's (2011) *Absorb, Do, Connect* approach to design activities that provided a mix of student engagement opportunities. In designing the first module, I decided to include *absorb* and *do* activities to familiarize instructors with the pace and goals. I included an introductory tutorial for passive learning (*absorb*) and then asked instructors to apply what they learned by taking a quiz (*do*). This proved a good time in the course design process for me to reflect on how effectively the activities supported the objectives. Organizing and rewriting objectives and activities is a messy process; however, it was worth investing the time to ensure well-organized materials that build confidence with instructors.

In order to assess the success of the Workshop, I customized a survey created by Arinto (2013), which was designed to assess instructor competencies for teaching an online course as basic, intermediate, or advanced. Participants chose all statements that applied to them across three areas: *content development* (e.g., I have updated my courses with library resources.), *design of learning activities* (e.g., I have written activity guides for library resources.), and *assessment* (e.g., I have written formative assessments for student's knowledge of library resources.).

Results indicated that the Workshop had helped develop basic instructor competency skills with online library materials. One example of basic skills is the way instructors used library tutorials in their own online courses. Rather than embedding them at the point of student need, most instructors listed research tutorials as supplementary materials in their online courses. This indicates that instructors may need more support and communication to include research tutorials in the most effective place. Assessment was the category with the fewest number of responses, indicating that most participants had not designed tests and quizzes to assess library skills. A new task analysis for assessment should be conducted in order to establish more support in that area for instructors. Moving forward, I have a stepping stone to focus future training around skills that would put participants in the intermediate skill area. Overall, this effort was met with enthusiasm and may lead to new instructor-library collaborations.

Bottom Line: By taking a train-the-trainer approach to creating course objectives and activities for the Workshop, I was able to capitalize on the research skills and instructional knowledge the faculty instructors already had while also building capacity for new library research objectives and tools within their online courses. The results of this case study indicate that the Workshop participants had developed basic competencies with online library materials. Moving forward, I have a stepping stone to focus future training around skills that would put participants in the intermediate skill area.

Administrators. Whether it is building library services into the common practices of their units, making sure librarians are involved in campus-wide efforts, or supporting library priorities, administrators can be great advocates for libraries as they direct their units and lead campus initiatives. Possible associates include:

- Academic department administrators
- Extension center directors
- International campus directors
- Provost or chief academic officers

Departments and services. Some goals require working with entire departments and services across campus. Any office that works with online students or manages online applications, networks, and systems is a natural partner for libraries. Possible associates include:

- Online learning office, instructional designers, and learning management system (LMS) administrators
- Tutoring and academic support
- Information technology departments
- Copyright office (if outside of the library) and legal counsel
- Academic advisors and counselors
- Accessibility services
- Campus web developer
- Marketing office
- Research support offices and institutional review boards

Outside the Institution

Other libraries. Pooling resources and services with other libraries, particularly those located closer to online students' geographic locations, may help the library connect with students. Possible associates include:

- Public libraries
- University and college libraries (both public and private)
- Community college libraries
- Technical college libraries
- Military libraries
- State and government libraries

Library-associated people and groups. Building a network of library staff who work with online students and online resources at other institutions can be very beneficial and informative. Through the collective efforts of librarians working with distance and online students, these partnerships may result in collaborative instruction, services, and (at a minimum) information sharing. Possible associates include:

• Other distance/online librarians in the region or state
• Library professional associations (e.g., the Association of College and Research Libraries' Distance Learning Section)
• Library consortia

K-12 schools. Connecting with local schools may help libraries connect with dually enrolled students and prepare incoming students for the rigors of college-level research. Possible associates include:

• Local high schools and middle schools (both public and private)
• Consortia or groupings of schools
• Local homeschooling associations

Businesses. Some goals require engaging with the businesses that provide resources that are used in the library's work online, while others may require libraries to reach out to local businesses and learn of their workers' information-seeking needs (particularly for libraries who want to tailor research instruction around lifelong research needs). Possible associates include:

• Publishers
• Third-party software vendors
• LMS companies
• Local businesses

Compare your goals and improvement needs with the possible associates inside and outside your library and institution. Who are the most logical partners? Narrow down the list to those with the most potential to be partners on a project.

Approaching a Potential Partner

When reaching out to potential partners, it is important to approach them with their needs and yours in mind. The first communication to the potential partner (whether an e-mail, phone call, or meeting) may take the following approaches:

• Requesting information about their services, goals, needs, and so on
• Requesting to learn about them by observing their work/department or joining their meetings

- Expressing interest in their work and requesting to brainstorm possible partnerships
- Explaining your ideas for a partnership, emphasizing how it might benefit them
- Explaining your ideas for a new or improved program, service, and so on and asking whether or not they are the most appropriate person with whom to discuss it

A combination of these approaches may also be appropriate, depending on how much you know of their goals and needs and what next steps you are proposing.

Depending on their responses to your questions and their level of interest, have an initial meeting (either in-person or virtually) to learn more about their needs and to discuss the partnership options. Clarify at the initial meeting (or set of meetings):

- What you and the library have to offer
- What they have to offer the library
- What gaps in their work you may be able to fill and vice versa
- What your current goals are for approaching them
- What their goals might be with this new partnership
- What needs you and they hope to address

Although you need to make it clear what you are able to provide and what you might need from them, be ready to discuss many possible types of relationships, collaborations, and partnerships. They may have different needs than you suppose and require different resources from the library than you were initially planning. Brainstorming at this stage is key to learning about each other, so use the brainstorming process to consider their needs and whether or not they complement your own. Move forward with relationships that work well for both parties.

Case Study: "Wait, There's a Distance Learning Librarian?"

Andrea Hebert, MLIS, Human Sciences, Education, and Distance Learning Librarian, *Louisiana State University Libraries*

When I started as the distance learning librarian at Louisiana State University (LSU), I did not have a road map to navigate the various types of online learning programs or a list of campus stakeholders. My position had been unfilled for more than two years, and most people I approached were unaware that there had ever been a distance learning librarian.

Cold calls and e-mail were mostly ineffective, but when I met people away from the library and around campus, they were more open to talking about programs and plans. I started to place myself where strategic contacts were likely to be, and I began to build up my network and extend my reach across campus. I improved my odds of having serendipitous encounters by:

- Searching newsletters from LSU Online, the Faculty Technology Center, and departments with online programs to learn about events and lectures. I signed up and invited myself to these events. Twitter and Facebook are also great places to find this information.
- Joining open committees related to online learning. It's hard to say no to people who volunteer for committees, and other committee members are eager to make contacts.

Even if there is not an immediate opportunity for collaboration, I reach out as often (or in some cases, as early) as I can so people remember me between points of contact. For example:

- I send short notes of congratulations when online programs and faculty who teach online courses receive honors.
- I periodically check the university's job postings to learn about new positions for departmental online learning coordinators and LSU Online staff. Being one of the first people to welcome a newcomer makes a good impression.
- I keep my ears open for news about upcoming program changes and position openings that have not been announced. Advance knowledge gives me time to think about what I may be able to do for that program before it begins or how I can support new hires before they are in place.

Each contact I have with stakeholders increases my chances of collaboration. For example, after working several times with a faculty member's face-to-face class, I mentioned my additional role as the distance learning librarian; a few weeks later she contacted me with a request to help her online students with database access issues. It marked the first time that an online instructor had contacted me directly for help.

Another success built on the relationship I formed with one of LSU Online's instructional designers while he was enrolled in doctoral coursework. I introduced him to library resources and services he was unaware of even as a face-to-face student. When he became the lead instructional designer at LSU Online, we collaborated on creating a set of short videos about library resources and services that were embedded in the orientation modules for LSU Online students. These may seem like small victories, but my progress is steady and meaningful.

Once I establish contacts, it is easier to develop new ones. People are more responsive when we share a mutual connection. Universities are small communities—there are often only one or two degrees of separation between people. When I approach administrators, faculty, and staff, I make sure to mention any contacts we have in common. Once that connection is made, suddenly I am not some random librarian—I am the librarian who knows one (or several) of their colleagues. The chances of getting a positive response to my offers and ideas go up.

Bottom Line: Frequent and proactive contact with both program administrators and online instructors, awareness of developments and changes in online programs, and a focus on how I can help instructors and their online students have helped me build a network of key players in online learning at my institution. Relationship building doesn't happen overnight, but intentional cultivation of relationships pays off in the end.

Planning a Partnership

Once the two (or more) parties have established a connection and have agreed to build a relationship, there are several options when it comes to the types of relationships to build, from informal and casual relationships to project-based collaborations to more formal partnerships. Take the ideas generated from the brainstorming sessions and establish a set of shared goals and best possible outcomes for the relationship. The type of relationship needed will change based on the goals the library and partners are attempting to accomplish. These goals will then inform the next steps of the planning process.

Case Study: We're All Better Together: Cross-Campus Collaborations to Support Online Students

Sarah E. Fancher, MS, Library Director, *Ozarks Technical Community College, Hamra Library*

Ozarks Technical Community College (OTC) in Springfield, Missouri, is a large community college serving a total enrolled population of nearly

12,000 students pursuing general education (typically with an intention to transfer to four-year institutions) and terminal technical degrees and certificates. More than 25 percent of credit hours are currently attempted online. The college has noted that important metrics related to student success, including course completion rates and GPA, tend to be lower for these courses. An institutional priority is therefore to effectively provide academic support services to this student population. In this case study, we examine how relationships have been built with key campus stakeholders, including disability support personnel, instructional designers, and learning management system (LMS) coordinators to leverage strengths, extend the library's reach, and jointly perform outreach and disseminate information to instructors. We collaborate to facilitate accessibility, fair use, information literacy, and student achievement by embedding subscription resources into the online course spaces, publicizing the availability of an online librarian, and offering support for instructor professional development.

OTC began to experiment with an embedded librarian model in 2009, when a librarian first made herself available to participate in course discussions in the learning management system (then Blackboard) and respond directly to student e-mails. Focusing primarily on English composition and psychology courses with research components, this model has achieved approximately 10 percent penetration in online general education courses. I came on board as the new library director just as the college began a phased transition to a new LMS (Canvas) in the Fall 2016 semester. Since making connections on campus was at the top of my agenda, the atmosphere of excitement and trepidation surrounding the LMS transition appeared to provide a natural point of entry for conversations with stakeholders. I hoped to strengthen existing relationships and ensure a library presence in more online courses by engaging directly on a timely topic.

First, library staff met with LMS coordinators to receive training on Canvas, utilizing a sandbox to become familiar with its features as early adopters in advance of the campus-wide migration. I also participated in the college's six-week "ONL-101: Online Teaching and Learning" course, which is mandatory for all new online instructors and covers elements of online pedagogy as well as functionality of the LMS. By expressing interest in their work and offering to be available as a resource, I next obtained invitations to attend monthly collaborative meetings with the LMS coordinators, instructional designers tasked with supporting online instructors, and disability support personnel. While the library already had a strong reputation for providing service to students, forming relationships with staff helped to highlight how the library can be an internal resource for these departments, simultaneously advancing our own interests. As a result of those ongoing meetings, we have been able to include announcements on the default Canvas homepage, including a short "meet your online librarian" introduction, and reminders about the availability of online research consultations timed to correspond with research-heavy points in the semester. We also facilitated the integration of subscription databases into online course spaces, and helped to plan a series of Facebook Live sessions for faculty (also recorded for later viewing) on best practices for accessibility and universal design in online courses. We have also acquired assistive technologies (e.g., the UbiDuo, a device for facilitating communication with the deaf or hard of hearing), which are available for in-library use or short-term loan.

In summer 2017, a campus renovation and space reutilization project had relocated the online instructional designers into a suite that is connected to the library. We hope that this physical proximity will continue to strengthen our relationships in support of online faculty and students. The instructional design team regularly hosts "lunch and learn" sessions for faculty to introduce new educational technology tools and to informally brainstorm how they might be implemented in various disciplines. We attend these casual sessions with the dual purpose of learning new tools and meeting faculty members. As a result, library staff have been invited to promote underutilized subscription resources that support pedagogy and facilitate professional development sessions for instructors. For example, one session on fair use has already been presented and recorded. Discussions among faculty on evaluating and adopting open educational resources, which are thought to positively influence student retention, are also taking place. Finally, in November 2017, a new instruction librarian was hired, and one of her initial project goals involves the creation or adoption of information literacy modules that will be made available in Canvas Commons and deployed in various courses. The instructional design team has been instrumental in helping to plan and produce tutorial videos, and in making introductions to faculty members who welcome instructional collaborations.

Although it is too soon to assess the full impact of these varied strategies on student success, there is an enthusiastic sense that momentum is building and that the library's interests are being advanced through partnerships with OTC Online and Disability Support Services personnel. Willingness by library staff to participate in conversations with these interested parties about issues of mutual concern has opened the door to increased collaboration, cross-referrals, and shared expertise. By engaging as enthusiastic allies, we have begun to reframe the library as a partner for faculty and staff in addition to a resource for students.

Bottom Line: It has been immensely fruitful to build relationships with staff from various parts of the college who also support faculty members' instruction in various ways. By connecting on shared interests, we have been able to leverage our respective expertise and open doors to conversations and collaborations that might not be possible if we were limiting ourselves to library outreach, without the benefit of strong allies. We have been reminded of the saying "if you want to go fast, go alone; but if you want to go far, go together."

Goals and Relationship Types

Instruction

With this type of relationship, librarians collaborate with faculty at their institution or at partnering institutions to provide information literacy or related instruction to students in specific courses. A common example of this type of relationship is embedding library-made instruction modules, videos, and assignments into an online course in the learning management system. Other examples include the development of instruction-based research guides for specific courses and publicly available research guides to which instructors can point their students. Libraries may also work with others including online student advisors and global campus and extension center directors on instruction and library orientation projects. The ultimate goal of such collaborations is to build library instruction directly into the online educational environments where students are learning, placing the instruction at the point of need and making it more easily accessible. See Chapter 6 for more detail.

Services

With this type of relationship, librarians work with a variety of partners, both internal and external, when providing shared services. Departments within the library find the user experience greatly improved by streamlining the processes through which users find, retrieve, and request library material. For example, if the library has multiple online forms for requesting interlibrary loan material and requesting home delivery of library material, perhaps the library could merge the forms to make things simpler for the patrons. Libraries could also connect with online students' local libraries and support those libraries' efforts in providing reference services, offering training on the databases unfamiliar to the local library. When looking at improved library services, the goals of such collaborations are twofold: (1) make the website and online resources (e.g., catalog and databases) as user friendly and easy to use as possible and (2) engage with students' local resources where they may be seeking research help as an alternative to using their institution's library.

Collections

Partnering with other libraries may also include sharing collections. For example, a university library may place select material in a community college library or a public library as a form of course reserves for online students located near the college. Library staff also partner internally with their special collections departments and archives in marketing and teaching the use of digital archival collections. These special collections and archives may be of particular use to select disciplines across campus, and libraries should prioritize the digitization of these resources to make them more accessible and to increase their usefulness to online students. Libraries also commonly join library consortia (e.g., the Greater Western Library Alliance and Ohio-LINK) that allow them to pool their resources and negotiate with publishers to license online content, particularly databases. The goals of these collaborations include increased access to library material, locating items where they may more easily be picked up, marketing specialized online resources, and acquiring/digitizing more content.

Programming

With this type of relationship, librarians seek out opportunities to be involved with campus programming for online students. A key program to identify and integrate into is the institution's new student orientation or new online student training, which may include modular introductions to services on campus and best practices for online learning—a great place to highlight library services. Also, the library should be a part of campus tours for visiting online students, particularly if the visiting students are dually enrolled high school students coming to campus on a field trip. These students, who may take a combination of online and in-person courses at the high school, often come to campus to get student identification cards and visit campus offices where they can receive help, including the library. Another initiative may include non-course-related webinars and online speaker series. If the library hosts speakers, record these events and stream them (with permission) for online students. The goal of such relationships is to introduce the library to new and visiting students and to provide equitable access to enrichment activities for online students.

Training

With this type of relationship, libraries work with both on-campus and off-campus groups to provide professional development opportunities to online faculty, staff, and students. These types of collaborative efforts can focus on campus initiatives such as increased use of open educational resources, improved instructional design, or accessible digital content. Partner with the campus's center for teaching and learning, distance or online learning departments, and accessibility services office to provide training on library services and resources. The goal of such collaborations is to encourage advocacy and marketing of libraries in their daily practice.

Case Study: Teaming Up to Support Online Patrons

Kathy M. Gaynor, MALS, MEd, Information Literacy Librarian and University Archivist
Holly Hubenschmidt, MLS, Head of Instruction and Liaison Services
Emily Scharf, MALS, MA, Head of Research Services
Webster University Library

Webster University began its online programs in 1999. Today approximately 37 percent of Webster students worldwide are enrolled in online classes. Webster's online programs are managed by its Online Learning Center (OLC). OLC works with academic departments to make courses and programs available online, and they provide support to students taking online courses.

We have provided library services to extended campuses since the university first took its on-ground programs to U.S. and international sites in the 1970s, so it was natural that we would expand our efforts to online programs. We now offer online students and faculty eBooks, streaming media, more than 150 databases, and support via phone, e-mail, or chat.

We have teamed up with OLC since its inception to make library resources and services easily visible and accessible to online users. Links to the library home page are fully integrated into our learning management system (LMS), currently Canvas. We have worked with OLC designers on library orientation and research instruction through text and video modules within courses, ranging from undergraduate general education to graduate capstones. The LMS allows librarians to be embedded into courses.

The library and OLC have also created instructional materials targeted to faculty. Due to the large number of adjunct faculty who teach in Webster's Walker School of Business and Technology, OLC, the Faculty Development Center, and Walker staff developed an online orientation course for adjunct faculty. We authored a module for this course, which discusses library collections, requesting materials, finding and using guides and tutorials, and getting assistance.

In 2013, OLC helped us develop a series of webinars for faculty and students. Today we offer presentations on wide-ranging topics such as APA citation style, finding tests and surveys, doing literature reviews, researching prospective employers, and support and resources for faculty research. The OLC continues to promote our offerings.

The OLC involves us in worldwide outreach to online students. For new online student orientation, OLC and the library collaborated on content for a module, which includes information on finding the library's website, a video made specifically for online students by librarians titled *8 Reasons to Use Your Library*, and instructions for finding resources and getting help. We regularly contribute to OLC's blog, writing articles about using the library that include information about research strategies and library services. OLC's Online Student Orientation and Support Specialist often shares social media posts from the library, and library news items are included in Constant Contact newsletters sent to students by OLC.

An important feature of the OLC-library partnership is the use of the OLC Commons, a discussion area in the LMS that allows online students to post questions. Initially, OLC staff would refer research-related questions to one of the instruction librarians to develop a response that the OLC staff member would later post. It quickly became obvious that the more efficient and time-sensitive method was to embed a librarian in the Commons. Now when a student posts a research- or library-specific question, we can reply directly.

OLC staff and librarians also work together to address the needs of students who appear to be struggling in their online courses. Students identified as "at risk" due to difficulties in understanding how to research are referred to librarians who contact these students through chat, phone, or e-mail. This joint OLC-library program provides individualized support to help students continue to make progress in their studies.

As work with OLC increased, library and OLC managers connected the staff of the two units to strengthen relationships, facilitate communication, and improve overall service to students. For example, we visited OLC offices to better understand their operations and workflows. Later, two OLC administrators led a project management workshop for library staff.

With the support from library and OLC management and ongoing collaboration among our staffs, we have been able to extend our partnership beyond traditional features like adding instructional content and embedding a librarian into the LMS. Through coordinated use of orientation modules, communication outlets, diagnostic referrals, and webinars on timely topics, we reach users at their point of need and take a proactive approach to addressing their issues.

Overall much of our success stems from a holistic approach to our services, providing research support from the time students begin their studies through the end of the course and program. We can also attribute our success to the fact that our units overlap very little in their core functions. We leave the course design to OLC, and they leave the information literacy to the library. Leveraging the relationship built over the years has empowered us to serve students better and understand what each partner can bring to the table.

Bottom Line: Webster University Library and the university's Online Learning Center (OLC) take a holistic approach to providing support to online students and faculty throughout an academic program. Those new to the university are provided orientation modules, and webinars on timely topics are offered throughout the term. The library and OLC collaborate through social media to promote resources and services and address questions posted to a forum for online students. Students struggling with research in their courses are flagged and referred to librarians for individual assistance. Overall, the library and OLC minimize overlap in their core functions and maximize communication and cooperation among the two staffs.

Formalizing the Partnership

As the partners further develop their relationship goals, the final planning steps include clarifying what each party will do to accomplish the goals, building a timeline, developing assessments and evaluations, and creating formal statements of agreement, if necessary. Although more informal relationships may require less documentation, having such documents may prove helpful should the relationship develop into something greater or when the partners need to report the results of their efforts to the library or campus administration or to the larger professional community.

Project Management

After clarifying goals of the partnership the parties should agree on a timeline for the various steps of their joint project. This is the time for the partners to establish committees, task forces, or other working groups as the project demands. The outline and timeline might include:

- Official first steps to get the project started
- Regular communication points when the partners report their progress to each other
- Dates and times for reporting to external stakeholders
- Steps for assessing the impact of the project on the established goals
- Steps for getting stakeholder feedback on the project
- Pivot points where the group reviews the project and considers changes

Only the most informal partnerships need not have the preceding information written down (e.g., when two departments promise only to refer patrons to the other party when appropriate).

Official Agreements

The most formal documentation between disparate parties is an official agreement, often called a memorandum of understanding (MOU). This type of document is often necessary when financial resources are involved, though sometimes contracts are more appropriate (e.g., when joining a consortium). A simple MOU often includes:

- The purpose, scope, and background of the partnership
- The terms or timeframe of the agreement
- The responsibilities of the library
- The responsibilities of the other party
- Any legal, liability, or indemnity clauses
- Signatures of those with authority to enter into the agreement

When developing such a document for the partnership, be sure to add time for both parties' legal representatives to evaluate the document and for it to be negotiated as it moves through administrative approval. Although not all relationships need such a formal document, MOUs can clarify the partnership for all parties, create a means to formally negotiate the parameters of the partnership, and provide historical perspective as the partnership moves forward.

Assessment and Evaluation

Having assessed the user experience and evaluated the potential for improvement at the beginning of this process for finding partners, build into the partnership assessment of the outcomes (particularly when student learning is involved) and evaluation of the services, resources, or other features of the partnership. This information will be pivotal when the parties decide on next steps and possible improvements. When working with online and distance students, consider these common feedback collection methods: focus groups via videoconferencing, online surveys, formal advisory group of online students, user data, error reports, and usability testing. Refer to the other chapters in this book for additional assessment and evaluation methods in their respective areas.

Conclusion

Situating the library in the best places to assist online patrons requires building dynamic relationships with a wide variety of individuals and groups. Because they will not always come to the library and use its full services, building a network of relationships, collaborations, and partnerships is key to successful online patron services.

Marks of a Good Relationship

Successful partnerships have a few important characteristics. When beginning a relationship, library staff should have these characteristics in mind.

All relationships. These common characteristics of successful partnerships apply to all working relationships, whether informal or formal. All parties should:

- Consider the needs and goals of the other parties
- Clearly establish goals for the project or partnership that are based on the needs of both parties
- Make clear their expectations for the relationship to the other parties
- Maintain strong communication among all parties
- Develop a method for receiving feedback about the partnership and its work

Collaborations and partnerships. More formal partnerships may require additional work to make them successful. All parties should:

- Develop a project plan with clearly defined roles
- Structure the relationship into formal committees, task forces, and working groups as necessary
- Negotiate formal agreements, MOUs, and so on as necessary (particularly for relationships between multiple institutions)
- Assess, analyze, and collect data on the nature of the relationship for the sake of reporting and future improvements

Library staff who serve online patrons have many options for building relationships that support their work. Ultimately, libraries need to consider their strategic goals, identify possible associates, set up different types of relationships, and then work together toward these goals. Following these steps, libraries can expand their connections to both students and partners throughout the library, the institution, and the wider community.

CHAPTER EIGHT

Marketing Services for Online Users

Laura Bonella

Introduction

You may have created the best library collections and services the world has ever seen, but if their existence is unknown, patrons cannot take advantage of them. "If you build it, they will come" works in movies, but not in libraries, so you will need to develop strategies to get information to online patrons about what is available to them. In order to do so, you will want to assess your offerings, get a baseline for patron knowledge and use of your services and resources, develop marketing strategies, implement changes to address unmet needs, and assess your marketing activities.

Assess Availability

At the beginning of your marketing process, make a list of the resources and services available to your online patrons (also see Chapter 1). You will discover that many of them are not place-dependent, and you may have offerings used by your in-person patrons that it hadn't occurred to you to promote specifically to online patrons. These could include:

- Interlibrary loan services.
- Electronic access to your catalogs, databases, discovery layer, and eBooks and journals.

- Reference services and specialized consultations (e.g., copyright) via phone, e-mail, IM chat, or video chat.
- Online subject guides or other subject resources.
- Information provided in a learning management system (LMS).
- Services for instructors, including help creating information literacy modules and assignments for their classes, and providing information literacy instruction.
- Access to institutional subscriptions to online manuals, reference management software (e.g., RefWorks or EndNote), language learning programs, standardized test study materials, or other types of productivity software.

Determine Baseline Knowledge

Before developing a marketing plan for the services and resources you have identified, it is helpful to have a baseline idea of what collections and services your online patrons already know about and use. One way to collect this information is by conducting a survey. In the survey, you want to ascertain:

- Are patrons *aware* of particular collections and services?
- Do they *use* them?
- And if not, why not (what are the *barriers*)?

If your library, institution, or municipality does a larger survey (LibQUAL+, a senior survey, etc.), see if questions already are or can be included about online access to library resources and services.

Creating a Survey

You can also conduct a survey specific to your library resources and services. We recommend wording the questions in a way that allows the survey to serve as an assessment tool and a marketing tool at the same time.

Survey Questions

When constructing your survey, consider the most important services and resources that online users should know about, and create a question to assess awareness of each. For example, in a survey sent to our online population (Bonella, Pitts, & Coleman, 2017; Pitts, Coleman, & Bonella, 2013), we created a list of services and asked, for each one, if the patron was aware or not aware of the service, and if they have used it. Here are some suggested types of questions:

- Do patrons know how they can get help from a librarian?
- Do patrons know that they have access to online materials like databases, books, and journals? Do they know how to access and use them?

- Do patrons know how to access help or FAQ information on your website that is specific to online patrons?
- Do patrons know about interlibrary loan services and how to use them?

In addition to these questions, include space for comments. This will allow patrons to share with you reasons they aren't using your services and resources (other than being unaware of them), as well as other useful information. We received multiple comments indicating that the survey itself had made patrons aware of services they didn't previously know about. One faculty member commented "[I previously] did not encourage distance student use of library services, but this survey has expanded my knowledge of available services, and now I will."

Survey Distribution

In order to receive useful results, you will want the survey to be taken by as many people in your target audience as possible. Here are some suggestions for reaching online patrons:

- In an educational setting, target patrons who have taken online classes. Target patrons who are not living locally. Send the survey to patrons whose address information indicates that they don't live near your library.
- Place a link to the survey on your library home page, database page, eBooks page, help page, or any page targeting online users.
- To increase participation, offer an incentive for taking the survey, such as a chance to win a gift card.

Case Study: Surveying Our Distance Users

Laura Bonella, Academic Services Librarian and Social Sciences/
Education/Business Team Lead, *Kansas State University Libraries*

At Kansas State University Libraries, we created a survey to find out how much our online education students and faculty knew about our services. We chose to create our survey in a way that informed our users about our services at the same time we assessed their knowledge. Rather than questions, we wrote statements. For each statement, we asked students to indicate whether they were aware of the service and had used it, aware of the service but had not used it, or not aware of the service. For faculty we asked whether they were aware of the service and had encouraged students to use it, aware of the service but had not encouraged

Distance Education

Welcome to K-State Libraries! It is our goal to help distance learners be successful in their studies. We have developed many resources to help you, and all services available to local K-Staters are open to you as a distance learner.

YOU CAN:

- Access research **databases, search tools**, full-text online journals (**e-journals**), and **e-books** through **K-State Libraries' website**

- Use web-based **subject and course guides** as well as other resources on the Libraries' website

- **Receive print materials** (books, maps, journals) and physical media items (videos, music CDs) in the mail if you live outside Manhattan

- Use **interlibrary loan** to borrow materials not owned by K-State Libraries

- Obtain **help from a librarian** through online chat, telephone, text, or email

- **Schedule consultations** with librarians for in-depth research assistance on the telephone, via e-mail, videoconference, or IM. Call us toll free at 855-4KSULIB (855-457-8542)

- Use the "Library Resources" tab in many of your K-State Online courses. If your instructor has enabled this feature, you will find a library basics or course-specifc research guide

- Use **RefWorks** to keep track of resources and automatically generate references-cited lists

To learn more, please visit our **Distance Learning Services** web page or **Ask a Librarian**

KANSAS STATE | Libraries
UNIVERSITY

Figure 8.1 Handout for distance students.

students to use it, or not aware of the service. Here are some sample statements from our survey:

- Online learners can obtain immediate help from a librarian through online chat, telephone or e-mail during K-State Libraries' service hours.
- Our library has web-based help pages specifically for online students.
- Our library can mail its print materials (books, maps, journals, etc.) and physical media items (videos, CDs, etc.) to distance students.

We also provided space to write comments.

We wanted to reach as many of our online patrons as possible, so we worked with our online education office to e-mail the survey to everyone who had taken or taught an online class in the past year. In order to increase participation in our survey, we offered a chance to win one of three $25 Amazon gift cards.

After we discovered which services our patrons didn't know about, we created marketing materials to provide better information. These included a "Top 10" things to know for distance instructors and students. Figure 8.1 shows the handout for students, which was distributed electronically. We also updated a page on our website that explained services available for online patrons.

We worked with our online education office to distribute the materials. They sent our handout to all students taking online classes. We also worked with them to update and enhance the information about the Libraries that was on their web page.

We included information about services for distance students on many of our LibGuides, whether or not the class was primarily online. Figure 8.2 shows an example of a statement that appears on some of our guides.

For Off-Campus Students

Almost all of our electronic resources are available to you from off campus by using your eID and password to log on. We will also scan and email articles from journals that we own, or will mail you books from our collection or books or articles borrowed from other libraries through **Interlibrary Loan**. For more information about library resources for distance students, see our **Distance Learning** page.

Figure 8.2 Example of information provided in LibGuides.

For more detailed descriptions about our surveys and marketing efforts, see our article in the *Journal of Library Administration*, "How Do We Market to Distance Populations and Does It Work?: Results from a Longitudinal Study and a Survey of the Profession" (Bonella et al., 2017).

Bottom Line: Survey questions can provide information as well as discover information. Finding out what your users already know about your services can guide you in creating helpful marketing materials.

Acting on Survey Results

Creating New Marketing Materials

Your survey may reveal surprising results about gaps in your patrons' awareness of what is available to them. After you have determined the services and resources your online patrons do not know about, you will want to develop strategies for informing them of what they can access. Create concise, informative handouts about important library services.

In addition to general marketing about online services and resources, you can create marketing materials that highlight those for unique patron groups (e.g., those interested in genealogy), courses, or particular assignments. These can be distributed at the time of need and are more likely to catch the attention of your online patrons.

Creating Effective Marketing Materials

Before you create your materials, ask:

- Why will people use your services? Focus on the benefit they will receive.
- What do you want your patrons to do? Include a call to action. Effective call-to-action phrases for libraries are ones like: register now, contact us, go to our website, or try it now.

Design Tips

Command Attention

- Make the copy easy to read. Use bullet points rather than paragraphs.
- Use bold colors and professional quality photographs.

- Keep it simple. You only have a few seconds to grab your patron's attention, so don't confuse them with a complicated design or too many messages.

Layout

- Use only one or two fonts.
- Use white space. It improves readability, directs a viewer's eyes, creates a clean and refreshing visual effect, and allows the reader to focus on what's important.
- Don't use all caps or multiple exclamation points.

Images

- One strong image is better than many little ones.
- Use images that look like the people you want to attract.
- Choose photographs over illustrations, illustrations over clip art. Do not use amateur-looking clip art.
- Make sure images are a size that will not print out pixelated.

Content Tips

Headlines

- Create excitement—include the most compelling patron benefit.
- Grab attention with questions.
- Speak to an individual, not a group.

Copy

Your materials should entice people to take you up on your offer.

- Use words that trigger a positive emotional response such as *achieve, new, easy, results.*
- Avoid overused phrases and library jargon.
- Focus on what will make someone want to use what you are promoting.
- Talk about what is unique about your event or service.
- Show how it solves a problem.

Content adapted from: https://libraryaware.uservoice.com/knowledgebase/articles/94566-tip-flyers-and-posters.

Distributing Marketing Materials

After you have created your marketing pieces, determine ways that you can share the information with your online patrons. You can, of course, put information on currently existing library channels. These may include:

- Library web page. Consider creating a page specifically for online patrons about what is available to them.
- Library social media channels.
- Research guides (e.g., LibGuides). Consider creating a guide just for online patrons, or including a statement on other guides about online access and other services available to online learners.

Brainstorm ways that you can find partners to help you get information to online patrons. At a university, for example, an online student's instructor or the online education unit can often be their primary (or only) source of information. Consider the following:

E-mail:

- Send e-mails to instructors who teach online classes letting them know about available services and asking them to share with their students.
- If you have an online education unit, partner with them to share information about the library with their instructors and students via e-mail and social media.
- If you have access to patron demographic information, send an e-mail to patrons who don't have a local address.

Instruction:

- If online students go through an orientation—online, in person, or even through receiving packets of information—include the library in that orientation.
- Look for opportunities to be included in any teaching courses or seminars that are offered to online instructors.
- Incorporate library information into every course in your LMS.
- Collaborate with any other schools or branches whose patrons might be accessing your resources.

Creating New Services

Your assessment may also have revealed that some of your services and resources are not available to online patrons but should be. For example, you might want to investigate a service that will allow patrons to text from their phone for reference assistance, implementing extended help hours for patrons with different schedules, providing chat or video reference service, mailing books or other materials to patrons, and so on (see Chapter 9).

Assessing Marketing

After your new marketing efforts have been implemented, you will want to assess them. Without assessment, you can't be certain that your efforts are working. Despite this, a survey of more than 300 academic librarians (Bonella et al., 2017) discovered that 84 percent did not assess their marketing to online patrons at all (Figure 8.3).

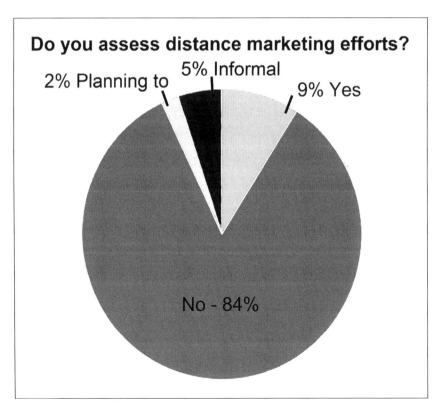

Figure 8.3 Results from a survey of more than 300 academic librarians.

There are several ways to collect information about the success of your efforts, for example:

- Periodically repeat your survey and compare results.
- Survey patrons about how they became aware of specific services so you can determine if they recall your particular marketing pieces.
- Determine if any of the following usage information is available and can be compared over time. If not, look for ways to gather it.

  - Views of YouTube videos
  - Statistics on use of your web page or research guide for online patrons
  - Number of information literacy sessions requested for online classes
  - Number of reference interactions via e-mail, phone, IM, or video chat
  - Number of online research consultations
  - Interlibrary loan requests

Even finding out that your marketing is not successful is useful information, because it gives you the chance to try something new.

Case Study: It's What Happens after Failure That Counts

Victoria Raish, PhD, MAT, Online Learning Librarian,
Penn State Libraries

We have all either created or inherited situations that were likely to fail. My failure occurred in the area of student outreach. Penn State Libraries have a very rich tradition of investing in student outreach and engagement beyond the classroom. However, this tradition was lacking when it came to our online students. As the online learning librarian for a population of 17,000 students scattered throughout the world ranging in age from young adult to retired senior, I feel an enormous duty to ensure that the American Library Association's (2016) standards for distance learners are met. Primarily, I think of *equivalent access* as a guiding principle in my work.

After assuming the role in January 2016, I set to work with ideas for how to reach students and provide them with access to and awareness of the libraries. Several of my initiatives were successful such as an interactive virtual library orientation and a research-focused embedded librarian program. However, one failure from my first year sticks out in my mind. Penn State has 24 physical campuses, including the large University Park campus. At University Park, we run a very successful and robust Open House. Approximately 3,000 students complete activities intended to introduce them to the library. In addition, several of our other campuses have an Open House. The online students did not have an equivalent introduction to the library.

I inherited an idea to invite online students in close proximity to a campus to visit their campus Open House. This idea stemmed from a valuable goal: to make our online students feel welcomed at our university. However, the initiative failed miserably. Not a single student visited a campus for their Open House.

There are a few reasons for this failure. First and foremost, we were not thinking of our student population when promoting this idea. Forty-four percent of online students live within the state of Pennsylvania, and thus many of them live in close proximity to one of 24 physical campuses. However, these students are still choosing online education for a reason. Many students choose online for flexibility, so it makes sense that they would not select a course load that requires being on campus at certain periods of time. Therefore, inviting them to an Open House with set times seems counterintuitive. Indeed, we were expecting online students to meet us where we are rather than meeting them where they are. Second, it was extremely complex to gather information on Open House dates and then effectively market this material. There was a misconception within our library that a relatively stable list of Open House dates existed. This turned out not to be the case. I spent a significant amount of time gathering information from each of our libraries as to when and where their Open House was located. Some of the campuses did not have a date for their Open House until shortly before the event occurred.

The marketing was also challenging. The team had to geographically target a small subset of the overall student population using specific details about the Open Houses. The marketing team does not want to widely promote opportunities that are not available to all online students, so this invitation was sent via e-mail communication to relevant students.

There was not an easy way to record attendance. The various campus Open Houses all collect information in different ways. Some of them have students swipe their ID card, while others simply count the number of students who attend. To have any sort of measurable indicator for the success or failure of inviting online students, numbers needed to be collected. While, for the most part, the campuses were able to add this workflow, it was an inconvenience for them when they were busy with several other more important aspects of the Open House and library operations.

At this point there were two options. I could accept this project as a failure and plan a different outreach initiative. Alternately, I could accept this as a failure and assume that online students did not want to engage with Penn State beyond their credit courses, and put less of a focus on outreach. Based on several data points, I was confident that the online students wanted a deeper connection to their university. Therefore, I chose the first option and brainstormed a more effective outreach program. In the new outreach program I wanted to prioritize student preferences and expand on a successful effort that the library already had in place. This led to the development of a "Blind Date with a Book" program for online students. This built on the residential program of the same name. In this program, students received a wrapped book in their preferred genre and were provided with instructions to share their book on social media. We worked with World Campus marketing and even before the form was widely advertised, we had 44 students signed up. This success was reassuring and taught me that it is what you do after a failure that counts.

Bottom Line: Online students have different needs than residential students. Residential programs do not always meet the needs of online students. In this instance, the first effort to provide equivalent access through invitations to residential Open Houses failed. It did not meet the needs and preferences of our students. However, utilizing data-informed decision making showed that students wanted a connection to Penn State beyond courses. This prompted a retooling of efforts and transforming another residential program that proved to be successful for the student population.

Although you may not be able to determine the physical location of patrons who use your resources, designing services that can be used by both distant patrons and local patrons who prefer to access the library online is beneficial (see Chapter 3).

Be Persistent

Keep in mind that your marketing efforts need to be continuous and sustained. Your population will shift as patrons move in and out of your service area (beginning and graduating from college, moving into and out of your city, etc.), and you will need to maintain your marketing efforts to reach the new patrons. Plan to regularly assess the success of your marketing, weed out anything that is not working, and implement new strategies to attract online patrons and make them aware of what is available to them.

CHAPTER NINE

Advocating for Your Online Users

Laura Bonella

Introduction

As a librarian who serves online patrons, make it a priority to advocate for what your users need. Your online patrons should have access to as many of the library's resources and services as possible. Earlier chapters of this book have discussed the details of how you can assess your services to online patrons. This chapter summarizes and provides additional resources for advocating for online patrons.

Planning for Change

The worksheet included at the end of this chapter (Table 9.1) can serve as a road map for assessing where changes are needed and the steps that you will have to take to implement those changes. You may download an editable version of this chart at: https://tinyurl.com/ch9chart. For each area, you will want to examine several questions:

1. What services or resources are currently available to your online patrons? Is their access the same or equitable to the access provided to in-person patrons?
2. In areas where the answer to the previous access question is "no," what needs to be changed?
3. Who are the decision makers who need to approve those changes—can you make them yourself, or do you need administrative approval?
4. Who is able to actually make the changes? Are technical skills required? If so, do you have the skills, or will you need to involve others?

5. How much of a priority are these changes? Are they significantly disadvantaging online patrons, or would they just be nice to have?
6. What resources are required to make these changes? Do you have the budget and staff time available?

Access to Electronic Collections

Libraries are devoting more and more of their collections budget to acquiring online materials. *The Chronicle of Higher Education* ("Average estimated share," 2017) reported that online journals, databases, and eBooks accounted for over 70 percent of academic libraries' materials budgets. Ideally, these materials can be accessed by all patrons at all times. Making choices that allow electronic materials to be more accessible to distance patrons can also benefit patrons who choose to use them from within the library. When planning for electronic collections, there are several issues to consider.

Licensing

When negotiating licenses for electronic materials, be sure that they allow for seamless access by remote patrons. If you are part of a larger organization or a consortium, your representative in that group should be ready to advocate for remote access. Consider the number of simultaneous users who are allowed. Ideally, this would be unlimited, but sometimes unlimited simultaneous users may be cost-prohibitive. If you are not able to provide unlimited access, track when patrons are turned away so you can assess the need for additional licenses. If you aren't already receiving this information, check with your vendors to see if it is available (e.g., through COUNTER reports). See the "Content" section of Chapter 10 for more on working with vendors.

Licensing Terms

Alice Eng, MSLIS, Electronic Resources Librarian,
Wake Forest University

Licensing of electronic resources is a daunting task, and you may be the lone librarian responsible for licensing. Most licenses contain consistent terms that define the user, outline how the resource can be used, and specify how the resource is to be accessed. Access for users who are physically present in the library is standard, but with universities expanding

---

their online presence and enrolling students globally, it is imperative that libraries negotiate licenses that include usage rights for online patrons and limit the liability of the library. Though not comprehensive, the following terms and clauses can impact online learners the most and should be included in your license. Create a checklist with terms that are most important to your library. It is a good tool to quickly evaluate whether you have what you require in your licenses. This is a very brief list. Work with your general counsel or the decision maker for your library for clarity regarding licensing.

Authorized Users

Definition: Students, faculty, walk-in users, people associated with the university.

What to clarify: Make sure the license allows your users to access the resource remotely. If a clause like this is not in the contract, you could be violating the terms even if your library requires authentication to access the resource.

Authentication

Definition: A type of identification process before the user can access the resource. Usually this is in the form of a secure page asking for a username and password from the patron or IP (Internet protocol) recognition.

What to clarify: IP authentication is preferred by most libraries since it is efficient for the library and user. Your library accepts the responsibility to create a secure method for only authorized users to view the resource's proprietary information by accepting this term. Although authentication adds a step for online students, it is a commonly used and easily understood security measure.

Learning Management System (LMS), Electronic Reserves, and Electronic Course Packs

Definition: These are the primary tools instructors employ to compile reading materials for online courses.

What to clarify: The contract should allow linking to or posting content from the resources in an LMS, electronic reserves, or electronic course packs. Ideally the contract will specify neither the amount of content that can be posted nor the length of time it can be made available.

Licensee Performance Obligations

Definition: Stipulations that the licensee agrees to uphold in terms of how the resource is used.

What to clarify: If not already included, this is a good area to add a clause or phrasing about libraries not being responsible for users' actions, only for making efforts to educate users about the terms of usage. Librarians cannot realistically police authorized users, especially those who are accessing resources remotely. The best a library can do is make users aware of usage terms. For example, a library can post a link for users to review the resource's usage terms.

Number of Users

Definition: How many users can access the resource simultaneously.

What to clarify: It is best to negotiate unlimited simultaneous users. However, that could be costly depending on the resource. If a resource is restricted to a specific number of simultaneous users, this could create access issues for a large class. Discuss with your vendor the possibility of lifting this restriction during certain times of the year like finals or if a class is working on a project for a finite amount of time. Those situations are not typically specified in contracts, but it is common for vendors to extend the number of users upon request.

Remedy Period

Definition: A period of time, defined or undefined, that you and/or the vendor have to resolve an issue. This can include situations such as the inability to access content from the vendor or unusual and inordinate downloading by a user.

What to clarify: Many times, a violation of the contract is grounds for a vendor to disconnect access to the resource. You want to avoid the provider abruptly disconnecting your access without warning due to a problem you were not aware of but that you could have resolved if you had been given the opportunity. This term should be in your license even if the length of time for remedy is undefined.

Connecting

Purchasing or subscribing to electronic materials is not useful if your patrons can't access them. Examine the potential barriers for online patrons to access your materials. Do you provide an easy, point-of-need method for patrons to authenticate into your resources? Best practice is to have a single sign-on, where patrons can use the same username and password for all resources. If they are having difficulty, how can they get help? What if the problem occurs outside of service hours? Try some of these ideas to help:

- Create an online page explaining solutions to the most common access issues.
- Provide ways—like browser tests—to help patrons ascertain where the connection problem is arising.
- Provide an easy way for patrons to report access problems. If possible, have someone assigned to respond quickly to these reports.
- Offer assistance via phone, e-mail, or other means to provide login assistance. Video chat can be helpful if you have a system that allows you and the patron to see each other's screens.

Case Study: Providing Technical Support to Online Patrons

John F. Coogan, MSLS, Electronic Resources & Systems Librarian
Kee-Young Moon, MS, MLS, Advanced Technologies Librarian
University of Maryland University College Library

The University of Maryland University College (UMUC) Library provides technical support for accessing online library resources to a community of over 86,000 students (including a large contingent of overseas and military students) taking online, on-site, and hybrid classes. This case study discusses the types of technical issues that our patrons encounter and our efforts to address them. We have developed a Technical Help section of the library website that includes pages covering login, browser, and connection issues, as well as problems with specific library resources. One-on-one assistance, provided by the Access Team, is also available.

Technical Help Page

The library's Technical Help page, which received over 3,300 hits during the past year, serves as a self-help starting point for patrons, bringing together the various tips and tools that we have developed for diagnosing and resolving technical issues. It covers the following areas:

Logging In

Login Help. The library now uses Single Sign-on for remote authentication, enabling patrons to use the same credentials for the library as for
everything else at UMUC. However, we still provide a page that
explains how to log in, tells patrons what to do if they encounter certain error messages, and offers an alternate "back door" login that can
be used if there are issues with Single Sign-on. Patrons can also submit a Login Problem Report form to request assistance.

Barcode Lookup. While most library resources now use Single Sign-on,
patrons still need to use their library barcodes to place holds on books
in the library catalog, so we have a barcode lookup tool that e-mails
patrons their barcode numbers.

Checking System Settings

In many cases, patrons have issues because of some settings or configu-
rations on their end. We have incorporated several tests that patrons can
click on to find out right away if there is a problem.

Browser test. This page runs a script that instantly tells the patrons
whether or not they have cookies and JavaScript enabled. There are
also links to instructions on how to enable these settings.

Firewall test. Patrons need to log in through EZproxy to access library
resources, but corporate and military firewalls are sometimes very
restrictive and do not allow access to proxy servers. (This can also
happen on home networks, but not as often.) As a result, when patrons
try to log in to library resources, they just get a blank screen. To help
diagnose this issue, we developed a firewall test. Patrons click on a
link that prompts them to log in to EZproxy, and if they are successful, they get a page that says "Congratulations." If they get a blank
screen or an error message, they can consult the Firewall page for
information that can be added to their firewall settings (or given to
their network administrators) to allow access to the EZproxy server.

Adobe Reader test. This page runs a script that instantly tells patrons
whether or not they have Adobe Reader installed, and links to the
Adobe site where they can download the latest version of Adobe Reader.

Satellite issues. Patrons who use satellite for their Internet service sometimes have an accelerator enabled, which makes web pages load faster
but can interfere with EZproxy. We do not have a test for this, but
suggest that satellite users turn off their accelerators to see if that
clears the problem.

Using Library Resources

Sometimes there are issues or anomalies with particular databases, and we post workarounds for these on the Technical Help page. We post notices in the Database A–Z list as well, when appropriate. We also offer a Database Problem Report form that patrons can use to notify the library when something is not working correctly. We report problems to the vendor and do our best to get them resolved at the source.

One-on-One Assistance

In addition to the self-help pages and tools listed earlier, two Access Team librarians, who work in systems, stand by to assist patrons when needed. Questions are initially fielded by the Reference Team. Technical questions get referred to the Access Team, who work with patrons via phone, e-mail, or WebEx. Using an online collaboration tool such as WebEx offers the option of seeing the patron's screen, which is very helpful in troubleshooting the issue and walking the patron through the steps to resolve it.

Access Team librarians evaluate the situation to determine whether the issue lies with:

- The patron's system (browser or network issues)
- The database vendor (search anomalies, content issues)
- Remote access (an EZproxy configuration is not correct)
- The online classroom (a broken link to a course reading)
- Single Sign-on (the patron's access has expired or is not yet activated)
- User education (the patron is confused about how to download an eBook)

Technical issues involving the patron's computer or network can be the most difficult to resolve, given that we do not have direct access to troubleshoot these. We point patrons to the appropriate tool(s) discussed earlier to help them narrow down the issue. Sometimes we need to go back and forth with them until there is a breakthrough, asking them to try different things and report back on the outcome. In best-case scenarios, we get to the root of the problem. Other times, we help the patron find an acceptable workaround to get what they need. And then there are times that we do not hear back and never know how things worked out. It can be a challenge indeed.

Bottom Line: We provide a handy technical troubleshooting checklist for patrons, including automated browser tests that will check their settings.

Discoverability

Your electronic resources will be used only if patrons can find what they need. When selecting journals or databases, consider how easy it will be for patrons to use them. Providing a discovery tool (e.g., Ex Libris Primo and SirsiDynix Enterprise) that allows patrons to search multiple resources as well as a link resolver that facilitates access to your electronic subscriptions will help patrons find and access the information they need. For more detailed information on this topic, refer to Breeding's (2015) "The Future of Library Resource Discovery" published by the National Information Standards Organization (NISO) https://www.niso.org/publications/future-library-resource-discovery.

Access to Physical Collections

Although electronic access to materials is becoming more prevalent, you will most likely have materials in your collection that are not accessible online—special collections, reserves materials, audiovisual collections, and others. Explore options for your online patrons to have access to those materials.

Delivering Electronically

For print materials owned by your library, set up a document delivery service to scan and e-mail articles or chapters to patrons. This workflow may be combined with the interlibrary loan process. Having this process be seamless for the patron—not requiring them to determine whether it is a request for scanning library materials or borrowing from another library—makes it much easier for them and more likely that they will make the request. If a patron can't access materials online, they can request the materials via one central form. The interlibrary loan team then either scans the library's copy if available, borrows it from another library, or purchases it when appropriate. Ideally, this will be available at the point of need; that is, the patron can connect directly to the form from the database or catalog rather than having to navigate to the form separately.

Delivering Physically

Your online patrons may need to use physical materials in your collection such as books or DVDs. In cases where copyright law does not allow making an electronic copy of the entire work to provide to the patron, you will want to explore ways to get the physical item to the patron. Here are some questions to consider:

- Which types of materials will you send to patrons?
- What service will you use to ship them?
- How will you track delivery and receipt?
- How will the patrons get the materials back to the library? In some cases, libraries have found it to be more cost effective to purchase the item for the patron to keep rather than asking for it to be returned.
- Who will pay shipping costs?
- Will you have a geographic range (e.g., only patrons in the United States, or will you ship internationally)?
- What will be the loan period? Will it be different from on-campus patrons? How will renewals be handled?
- What will be the fine policy?

Restricted Items: Many libraries have portions of their collection that do not regularly circulate outside of the building or have very short loan periods. This may include reserves, special collections, current periodicals, reference materials, or popular current literature. How can you provide access to these materials for online patrons, either by scanning on demand (where copyright restrictions allow) or by revising the policies for circulation? Of course, there may be situations where the condition of particular items or their value does not allow for access outside the library, but minimize these exceptions as much as possible.

Case Study: Service Excellence: Free Return Shipping for All Patrons Who Are Off Campus

Susan Powers, MLIS, Access Services and Resource Sharing Librarian
Melissa L. James, BS, Metadata Manager
Central Michigan University

Central Michigan University (CMU) is a public university that serves about 26,000 students. Our CMU Libraries interlibrary loan department, called Documents on Demand, is a relatively new unit that is the result of a merger between the former Distance Library Services department and the on-campus interlibrary loan office. The new department now serves all on-campus, distance, and online students, faculty, and staff.

CMU has a long history of supporting distance learners. The library has shipped materials to students since the 1920s. However, students were always responsible for paying for return shipping. In 2013, the Documents on Demand team proposed a pilot program to provide free return shipping to all of our patrons who were off campus, including students, faculty and staff in our Global Campus program, and those on internships or student teaching. The goal was to make library use more convenient for distance users, and to support academic success.

Selecting a Shipping Service

Before beginning this program, Documents on Demand shipped books the same way we ship interlibrary loan books to other libraries: through UPS ground service via our campus mailroom. This service was inconvenient for our patrons. We received complaints because delivery times varied widely. Deliveries estimated to take two to three days sometimes took five to six days to reach the destination. The time of day for delivery was also unpredictable. This was problematic because an adult signature was required at delivery. If no one was present to sign, the package would not be delivered. These issues prompted us to begin searching for a more reliable, user-friendly service.

We researched three main delivery options for the free return shipping program: United States Postal Service (USPS), UPS Express Services, and FedEx Express. We found that USPS tracking was not granular enough for our needs, and delivery times were still too unpredictable. The UPS Express Service provided the level of service that we wanted, but cost more, so we chose FedEx Express. FedEx Express provides several advantages:

- We get all packaging materials such as boxes, envelopes, padded bags, and plastic windows for shipping labels (known as waybills) at no charge, delivered to our office.
- Creating shipping and return labels is quick and easy online at fedex .com.
- We can generate a return shipping label and send it with the patron's material.
- If patrons lose their return label, they can contact us and we can e-mail them a replacement label.
- We have a fixed daily pickup window. FedEx picks up packages from our office directly, without us having to wait for items to go through processing at our campus mailroom.
- All packages are tracked, and we can opt to require a signature if a package's total value exceeds our threshold.

- In the event FedEx is unable to deliver a package, the packages are returned to us at our expense.
- In the case of a shipping error on our part, such as shipping to an old address, we can issue a "door tag" and recall or reroute a package to the correct location.
- FedEx gives a discount to educational institutions, so we pay a reduced rate for shipping.
- The fedex.com website offers reporting functionality on the current two years of transactions.

Initial Evaluation of the Pilot Project

It became clear early on that the new program was a success. We sent an informal, brief survey with our books asking patrons to give us their feedback upon return. All feedback was positive. Patrons loved the service and asked us to make it permanent. Our analysis of the pilot showed that we did not experience a large increase in the number of patrons requesting books from us, but the patrons who did use the service generally placed more requests. Costs were manageable: outgoing packages cost an average of $12.40, and patron returned packages cost an average of $9.48. The FedEx service itself was extremely efficient. All deliveries occurred on time as predicted. The FedEx customer service department even took the initiative to call us around national holidays to enquire about when our office would be open for business to make certain our items continued to go out on time.

The Service Today

The free return shipping program continues today, with only a few small tweaks. We no longer require patron signatures on delivery, because FedEx tracking is sufficient. We gave direct access to our fedex.com account to our business office, enabling them to reconcile credit card bills without needing to go through our office. We created a way to print our own simple "how to return your package" instructions on the back of the free return shipping label, so that the directions would not get lost. One of our patrons commented, "Thank you! This program is extremely helpful and convenient." We are glad we are able to support our users' research endeavors with this service.

Bottom Line: We piloted a free return shipping service for faculty, staff, and students needing physical library materials at off-campus locations. Feedback was positive.

Access to Services

Reference and Research Consultation Services

Your online patrons should be able to access reference and research consultation services in a way that is equitable to what is provided to in-person patrons. Phone and e-mail reference are easy to provide equitably to all. However, when planning research consultations, there are additional considerations to ensure that online patrons can take advantage of the assistance. Allowing patrons to schedule a reference consultation that will use video chat is a good way to provide this service. This can be done using free services such as Skype. To take the consultations a step further, your video chat system will ideally allow you to share your screen with the patron and vice versa. The technology should be easy to use on both sides—if the patron needs to download software or do a complicated setup, it may discourage them from using the service. Use a calendaring system that allows patrons to schedule their consultation time without having to speak to a staff person to do so, such as youcanbook.me. The more hours of service you can provide, the better. Where possible, provide phone, chat, or videoconference reference services even outside the hours that the physical help desk is open, particularly if you have a significant number of patrons who reside in different time zones or whose work schedules might make it difficult for them to access help during your traditional hours. Cooperative reference services are another way to extend your hours to meet online patron needs. Finally, staff should be trained in techniques for helping online patrons (see Chapter 4).

Instruction

Whenever possible, make your library instruction classes available to online patrons via videoconferencing. You can do this live, or by posting recordings of the classes, or both. If staffing allows, it is helpful to appoint an online facilitator who can monitor the videoconference, troubleshoot any access problems for online patrons, and relay questions they may have to the presenter. Also consider making short videos that are intended for self-paced viewing. This will benefit not only your online patrons but also any of your users who want to know more about using library resources. In some cases, having a librarian embedded in the class to provide instruction can be useful (see Chapter 6).

Programs

As with instruction, allowing online patrons a chance to benefit from your programming should be a goal. This can happen by either live streaming or recording your programs for later posting. Your library could have a YouTube channel where you share these programs, or create podcasts based on the programs.

Marketing and Outreach

Finally, your online patrons can't take advantage of services and resources of which they are unaware. In the previous chapter, we described how to conduct a marketing assessment. Do your online patrons know what services they can access? Does your marketing material make it clear that services are available to them? Do you have a connection with faculty who are working with online students? Creating effective marketing materials and working with partners to get service and resource information to online patrons will help ensure they use available services.

Sustaining Success

In our experience it is much easier to develop a successful system than it is to improve it or even to sustain it. After the excitement of new challenges begins to fade, it is easy to turn creative energies to other horizons. Fortunately, there are several strategies you can employ to ensure that your services for online patrons continue to meet their needs. We conclude with an overview of some of the most important of these strategies.

Continuously Explore User Needs

Your library's user population is constantly changing. New users arrive and some leave. Those who remain gain new skills, develop new interests, or take on new challenges. And all the while, technology and society evolve at a rapid pace. In order to ensure that the knowledge your library employees embed online and the skills they incorporate into proactive communications stay relevant, they will need to constantly refresh their understanding of their patrons' needs. The following techniques will help you stay up-to-date:

- Regularly examine search logs for your website, databases, discovery system, and frequently asked questions. While it is useful to examine each set separately, it is most important to combine these logs into a single group. Track changes in the queries over time. Rather than assign analysis of this combined file to one employee, turn it into a group exercise. The more individuals who see this information, the better off your users will be.
- Keep up with any changes in relevant patron demographics or characteristics that are collected by your library, institution, or organization (e.g., primary languages spoken, enrollment levels, age) that may indicate a need for changes in services. Demographic data by itself does not indicate how your patrons

will use your services, so use focus groups, surveys, and interviews to continuously update your understanding of your users and the context in which their information needs are embedded. Develop a schedule for conducting these explorations on an ongoing basis. Again, it is beneficial to spread this work among a large number of employees and share the information with all of the library's staff.

- Regularly examine the course offerings in the schools whose students your library serves. When new classes are developed, contact the instructor to learn about the information-seeking challenges those students will face. These conversations may reveal the need for new course or assignment guides to help students succeed. They may also help your library employees stay up-to-date on new trends in pedagogy and curricular goals.

Keep Up with Online Technology

Inevitably new communication, organization, and searching technologies will arise and influence the day-to-day experiences of your patrons. While we don't suggest that your library should strive to be on the leading edge of every new trend, we do feel that it is vital to catch up to those changes that become widespread. If you don't, the new users who encounter your systems may see them as outdated, outmoded, and irrelevant. The following are some of the most useful methods for keeping up with technological changes relevant to online services and resources.

- Become actively involved in communities of librarians who are interested in technology.
- Attend conferences and visit with vendors to learn about new products and innovations and to share information about the needs of your online patrons.
- Work with your librarians to develop a reading list and divide responsibility for staying current with the publications on the list. Establish an expectation that each member of your team will alert the group to articles or posts of interest.
- Explore other libraries' websites. Again, rather than assign this to one employee, we recommend dividing this responsibility among as many employees as possible. Develop a simple online form for them to complete for each website they examine. And ensure that the form has question prompts that direct attention to specific aspects of the site, such as methods for providing answers to frequently asked questions, types of course or assignment guides, and technologies for connecting patrons to library employees synchronously or through appointments.

Having a plan for sustaining changes and continuing development before you start implementing too many new strategies will ensure that you continue to provide the best service to your online patrons without putting too much stress on your staff.

Table 9.1 Advocacy plan.

Use this chart to create your plan for advocating for your online users. The first column lists access considerations. If your answer is "no," use the other columns to plan for change. Some example questions are already listed, and you can add your own as well. You may download an editable version of this chart at: https://tinyurl.com/ch9chart.

Access point	Circle one	Plan for change				
		What needs to be changed?	Who controls the decisions?	Who can make the changes?	Priority? (high/ medium/low)	Cost?
Licensing—all licenses for electronic items allow access by online patrons affiliated with the institution	Yes No	Do licenses allow enough simultaneous users for each item? Can patrons easily authenticate into the resources?	Library negotiations or through a consortium?			
Library collections—library-owned materials can be mailed to patrons	Yes No	Are charges to receive or return materials creating a barrier? Do materials arrive in a timely fashion? Is it easy for distance patrons to return materials? Do loan periods or fine policies need to be adjusted?				

(Continued)

Table 9.1 (Continued)

Access point	Circle one	Plan for change What needs to be changed?	Who controls the decisions?	Who can make the changes?	Priority? (high/medium/low)	Cost?
Library collections—special collections, reserves, audiovisual, and so on are accessible to distance patrons	Yes No	What processes are needed to scan materials or otherwise ensure access for distance patrons?				
Document delivery—scans of library-owned materials can be sent to patrons electronically	Yes No	Can patrons easily request these materials at the point of need?				
Interlibrary loan/document delivery—it is easy for patrons to figure out how to request materials	Yes No	Do you have one central request form, or does the patron have to decide which form to use based on the kind of material they need?				
Library or organization's IT—online patrons are able to easily authenticate to use library materials	Yes No	Access for international patrons? Patrons behind firewalls?		Do you need to work with campus IT?		

Library services—online patrons can receive help via phone, e-mail, chat, or videoconference with service levels and hours equal to those available for in-person patrons	Yes No	Do service hours work for online patrons? Do you need to extend hours? Do you have access to appropriate software for chat and videoconferencing? Is the software easy to use without extensive technical knowledge?		Can you purchase software that allows screen sharing?
Library services—it is clear to online patrons that help is available to them and how to request it	Yes No	Is there a clear link on the home page, databases page, catalog page, or other heavily used pages to get help?		
Library services—library staff are trained to work with online patrons	Yes No			
Library services—instruction classes and programs are accessible to online patrons via videoconferencing or later viewing of recordings	Yes No	Will you need an additional instructor to answer questions from online patrons?		

(Continued)

159

Table 9.1 (Continued)

Access point	Circle one	Plan for change — What needs to be changed?	Who controls the decisions?	Who can make the changes?	Priority? (high/medium/low)	Cost?
Library services—faculty who teach distance patrons know about library services and share with their students	Yes No					
Marketing/outreach—distance patrons are aware of services and resources that are available to them	Yes No					
Accessibility—online materials and services are accessible to patrons with disabilities	Yes No	Are materials able to be read by screen reader programs? Is information conveyed without relying on color? Do videos include closed captioning?				

	Yes / No			
Accessibility—online materials are designed so that they do not require excessive bandwidth to use and are a reasonable length	Yes No			
We have a plan for assessing and updating our services on a regular basis	Yes No			
We have a plan for continuous training and improvement of staff skills	Yes No			
Other:	Yes No			

CHAPTER TEN

Online Access to Public Library Services

Adam Wathen

Public libraries incorporate much of what has been discussed in previous chapters into the online services we provide. Similar to academic libraries, public libraries assess library services and community, set goals and measure those goals, examine design and incorporate universal design principles, provide online reference services and content, and market our resources. In this chapter, we focus on online discovery, content, and programming and outreach services in the public library.

Access to information is often considered to be the primary objective of libraries. Access is a very broad mission for public libraries because they serve a patron base that encompasses all members of the community. This includes patrons of any age, ethnicity, language, religion, experience, education, and financial status. This likely even includes patrons who don't have a library card or are not residents of the library's service area. The breadth of this patron base creates unique hurdles for the public library and drives many of the solutions described next.

Discovery

Discovery is the path for our patrons to get access to information. Public librarians use a wide variety of online discovery tools to connect patrons with resources they are seeking. Like the academic library, the public library provides discovery actively through reference services and passively through tools, guides, and metadata that lead patrons to the information they seek.

Providing online reference services is convenient for patrons, but it is an expensive option for libraries as it often requires staffing an additional reference service point. To provide online reference, libraries integrate specific communication tools like chat, instant messaging, video chat, text, social media, and phone services into the web interface of the library. Promote any online reference service you provide with clear hours of operation and clear instructions. You might also choose to use asynchronous reference tools like e-mail. Asynchronous tools can be useful to deliver reference services without the expectation of immediacy that allows the library the flexibility to dedicate staff resources when it is convenient for the library while still meeting patron expectations.

As with all services you are providing, you need to evaluate the way you are delivering online reference. Begin by determining what your goals are for the service. Measure how well the service meets your goals. And don't be afraid to change how you are delivering a service or even stop the service if it isn't effectively meeting your goals. For example, if you find that chat reference is rarely used and isn't easy to use, it might be using resources that could be dedicated to a more effective service for patrons. You might find that you provide better service by reducing the number of technological paths to reference service, which might reduce information overload for patrons. On the other hand, you may find that your patrons desire multiple pathways and multiple technologies to access reference services.

When you assess these services, take advantage of the resources available through the Public Library Association's Project Outcome. Project Outcome provides "a free online toolkit designed to help public libraries understand and share the impact of essential library programs and services by providing simple surveys and an easy-to-use process for measuring and analyzing outcomes" (Project Outcome, 2019). You will find survey and data tools that will make it easier to measure and report the value of your services. You may still need to create specific measuring tools in order to answer targeted evaluation questions like whether IM chat reference would work better for your library than text reference.

Also similar to academic libraries, public libraries curate passive subject guides for patrons to discover the resources they might be seeking. Be strategic in the creation and curation of these guides. Ensure that the guides you produce have the ability to remain relevant to your community for long periods of time. Add value in the guides you create by directing patrons to unique, local, and purchased content. For example, a genealogy guide might provide links to local obituaries and cemetery records and provide instructions on how to access library-subscribed genealogy databases.

Assess online guides in a similar way that you would assess your collection. One way to do this is to apply an adapted version of the CREW "MUSTIE" Method (Larson, 2012) that asks you to evaluate if the content is:

- Misleading or factually inaccurate
- Ugly—in an online environment this factor is less relevant but could be applied if the content is not in a format that scales on different devices or if the web pages have significant amount of annoyances like ads, pop-ups, or redirects
- Superseded by new information or a much better source
- Trivial—of no discernible literary or scientific merit
- Irrelevant to the needs and interests of the your library's community
- Elsewhere—the content is easily obtainable in a general web search

Every community is different, and you will have to understand your community to determine what content is valuable. See Chapter 4 for further discussion, more examples, and case studies of online reference services.

One area of reference that remains largely in the public library sphere is reader's advisory. While public libraries actively perform reader's advisory services through the reference services detailed earlier and in Chapter 4, recommendation lists are a strong alternative. You can use a variety of channels to deliver reader's advisory services. You can directly target patrons by sending recommendations through e-mail, or you can broadcast recommendations through social media, radio, or television. Reader's advisory can be effective as a passive tool to be found when patrons need it. Embed recommendations in catalog lists, blogs, online videos, or podcasts. Examine patrons' behaviors to determine how they might best connect to your reader's advisory services. Design your online recommendation pathways around your objectives and how your patrons connect with you. It might be better to deliver book recommendations through a local radio show if you are intending to increase the community awareness of and confidence in the library. However, if your goal is specifically for library power users to access recommendations, then in-catalog options might be more effective. Don't be afraid to provide the same recommendations in multiple spaces to accommodate many user preferences.

In addition to traditional library catalog records and MARC record metadata, most library catalogs now provide integrated tools to enhance reader's advisory by allowing users and librarians to create lists, recommendations, reviews, and content tags. The limitations of subject headings to effectively lead patrons to the content they are seeking should drive you toward taking advantage of these tools. In addition to making these tools available for patrons where you can, leverage the expertise of library staff by creating reviews and tags in your online catalog.

Library catalogs also offer convenient online spaces for patrons to be able to manage their library experience, seek information, access content and library services, and control and archive their searching. Some catalog interfaces have even come to the point where they allow patrons to view content (eBooks, eAudiobooks, and streaming content) in the frame of the catalog.

Make these self-management and self-directed tools a high priority in your evaluation of your catalog. Engage your patrons in the discovery of information by letting them curate their own content lists and engage with you in dialogue about the content they use.

Extending the searchability of your catalog depends highly on leveraging metadata content to supplement the MARC record. Look for ways to integrate third-party and patron-created content into your web catalog to enhance the library records. Providing the opportunity for patrons to add reviews, subject tags, lists, comments, and other content is a valuable way to not only engage your patron base but also to create an additional layer of information for your patrons to understand the content being described in the catalog record. Third-party catalog enhancements can add a host of information to enrich catalog data like reviews, tags, similar titles, library maps, awards, and Lexile data. Assess which added content would be valuable to your patrons. While it might feel attractive to add all of the information options you can to a patron's search experience, it is important to be judicious so you don't overwhelm the patron by adding complexity that might end up interfering with their ability to self-navigate the library.

Content

Public libraries have significantly increased the amount and variety of online content available to patrons over the past 10 years. Now, it is expected of public libraries to provide online access to reference resources and databases, books and audiobooks, magazines and newspapers, music and video, and training and educational resources. Navigating this space in the public library means working within a complex arrangement of vendors, contracts, rights management, authentication, and resource evaluation. Chapter 9 details many of the ways libraries engage with vendors to advocate for access.

In public libraries, providing access often means negotiating with vendors to make their proprietary content available to a large and often-nebulous user population. Make sure you understand the scope of your user base. What are the geographic or political boundaries you use? What are your policy restrictions on who can obtain a library card? Do you share online access with other libraries or organizations in a consortium? Do other libraries share your catalog that grants access to online resources for their patrons?

Consider the ways you intend to provide access to online resources and make those explicit in your contracts with vendors. You and your vendors will need to agree on how you control access in order to comply with their expectations. Be explicit with vendors about how you intend to share their content, what the scope of your user base is, and any organizations that you intend to partner with or give access to. Access to vendor-supplied content is legally limited to the user base defined in your contract.

To control patron access, vendors utilize several authentication and delivery models, each with different implications for public libraries.

- Seats or metering: Vendors may limit the number of patrons who have access to content or the amount of content a patron can access. Pay close attention to the patron experience. Being blocked from access because other patrons are using an online resource or having a long wait in a holds queue are experiences that might significantly reduce the value of the resource for your patrons. As well, metered access (e.g., only being allowed a certain number of uses per month) can produce a patron experience that is frustrating or disincentivizes returning to the service.
- SIP2 authentication: Libraries rely on SIP2 (Standard Interchange Protocol) regularly for interface between systems, but it is largely a library-only protocol. Vendors who are entering the library marketplace may not have integrated SIP2 authentication in their products. In addition, SIP2 does not include any encryption options, and vendors might be unwilling to authenticate through SIP2 when their data is at stake. Be willing to consider alternatives if this is a problem for a vendor.
- Vendor-controlled user accounts: Some products require that users have individual accounts with the vendor in order to access content. This may be the case when a vendor first enters the library market because this is the direct-sale model they used in the direct-to-consumer marketplace. Turning over patron data to vendors in this way may mean that the library loses the ability to manage the patron experience as the account is controlled and possibly owned by the vendor. In these instances, it becomes easier for vendors to upsell to patrons directly, to market to patrons, or to sell patron data. Be wary of vendor-controlled user accounts and add language to the contract that limits the vendor's ability to use patron data in ways that abridge patron privacy or violate confidentiality policies.
- Library-only use: Some vendor products are limited by contract to be used only inside the library on library computers. The value to online patrons is severely limited in these instances since patrons must be in the library building to access the online resource. Also, multilibrary systems or consortial systems must be careful in implementation as it is sometimes the case that a contract limits access to a single building and the implementation has allowed broader access. Wherever possible contract in ways that include online patrons.
- Pay-per-use: One of the recent innovations in access to online library materials is directly charging the library for each patron use of material. This could be a valuable solution for a library that anticipates low use or online access to materials as a limited supplement to other collections. The return on investment for pay-per-use is static as the library is assessed a flat cost for every use.

Because of this, a library is forced to limit the resource based on allocated budget. The more use a service gets, the more cost to the library. This incentivizes libraries to limit patron usage. On the other hand, an unlimited use model (like the commercial services Netflix or Hulu) increases return on investment the more patrons use it, decreasing the cost per use as usage increases. There are few unlimited use options for eBooks and streaming content for online content in the public library market. Evaluate the economic impact on the library for the number of patrons you are serving.

Public libraries, like academic libraries, continue to migrate local material to online repositories and databases. Patrons have benefitted from this increased online access to rare and locally relevant materials. For example, many public libraries provide online access to local collections such as photos, yearbooks, newspapers and magazines, music, film, and cemetery or obituary information. This function often overlaps with the mission of other local cultural institutions like museums, archives, historical and genealogical societies, and academic institutions. Explore how you can enter into partnerships to create access to this content and introduce it to a broader audience.

As with any of the services provided to online patrons, think about evaluation and usage reports. Make sure that the evaluation information you are getting from your vendors is the information you need to determine if the service is working for your patrons.

Programming and Outreach

Public libraries offer many activities, events, and performances inside the library and services delivered to targeted audiences outside of the library. These services are most often still physical and are not easily replicated for the online patron. You may find that few library programs can or should transition to the online space. Assess how your patrons want to access your programming and what outcomes you want. Some but not all of those outcomes may be achievable in the online space.

Libraries have successfully created alternate online versions of programs like book clubs, but most programs remain solidly in the physical space for public libraries. One reason may be that the outcomes of much programming demand engagement that is more easily achieved in person than online.

Online programming often ends up being asynchronous, delivering training or content to patrons through digital video or audio. For example, libraries offer video recordings of staff performing children's songs, stories, or puppetry. Libraries also offer recorded online tutorials that are similar to content delivered in how-to workshops. Another example is Los Angeles

Public Library Foundation's long-running "Stay Home and Read a Book Ball" where its foundation encourages people to stay home, read a book, donate to the foundation, and connect with other at-home readers on social media. And, in 2017 Cincinnati Public Library launched a recorded phone-based storytelling service. This service has been a standard in some libraries for more than 40 years (Crowley, 1990).

It is much more prevalent to see libraries enhance the programming offered in the library by using technology to increase access or value. A debate, lecture, or author interview held at a library could be simultaneously live-streamed on social media or recorded for later viewing. An art exhibit could be represented online. These kinds of online experiences are not the same as physical attendance, but can serve patrons and meet your objectives. No matter how you deliver this content, ensure that your outreach and programming have clear and discoverable pathways on your web page so that patrons are informed of specialized services and the ways to take advantage of them.

You will also find value in augmenting your programming and outreach with online tools that allow patrons to engage with those programs in more ways than just attendance. For example, use social media channels or an online forum for discussion around an event, or use online spaces for social editing and review in patron writing programs.

Many of the recommendations in this book for academic libraries are valuable in the public library space as well. Depending on your patron base and the other resources available to patrons in your community, you can provide online services that utilize the same techniques as academic libraries. It is important to understand your community and be responsive to it. Create online services that solve patron problems, but use caution so you do not accidentally add unnecessary barriers to patron access. Regularly review the efficacy of the solutions you implement. In a quickly changing technology and information environment, patron needs and behaviors shift and your library solutions need to be ready to respond to those shifts.

Conclusion

In the preceding 10 chapters and 23 case studies, some two dozen librarians have presented a variety of techniques, theoretical frameworks, models, technologies, and best practices to enable you to provide your online users with exceptional services. Rather than describe a utopian system, we intentionally focused on the practical and attainable. And in recognition of the vast disparities among libraries in terms of resources and populations served, we strove to present alternative techniques for meeting common user needs and to emphasize guiding principles that could be applied to situations we failed to imagine. At the same time we sought to clearly identify minimal acceptable levels of service. We did so by noting nearly ubiquitous policies, technologies, and service offerings. We worked hard to strike the right balance between generalizability and specificity.

As authors of a practical manual, we were particularly keen to ensure that the book would have value for many years. For that reason we elected to have the 10 chapters address topics we anticipate will be relevant to libraries for as long as organizations with that name continue to exist. As long as libraries endeavor to use their resources to help patrons access and create information and as long as patrons wish to avail themselves of services and resources from innumerable locations within and external to physical buildings, they will need to plan (Chapter 1), assess (Chapter 2), design (Chapter 3), and market (Chapter 8) those services. They will also be focused on ensuring that their patrons have access to expertise to help them overcome access challenges, conceive effective search strategies, choose wisely among numerous search results, or find the perfect story for inspiration. To this end, they will want to create methods to reach individuals actively and passively in both reaction to needs and anticipation of future information needs (Chapters 4, 5, 6, and 10). To the extent that they continue to license resources, they will need to license the resources to ensure maximal benefit to patrons, both local and remote (Chapters 9 and 10). In order to accomplish these goals, they will need to form partnerships (Chapter 7) and successfully make the case for expenditures to administrators or directors (Chapter 9).

You likely noticed that nearly every chapter and many of the case studies stressed goal setting, user needs analysis, and assessment techniques. Several advocated for universal design to meet the needs and abilities of as wide a variety of individuals as possible. And many noted that while each separate service, page, or object should be created with universality in mind, there should be sufficient flexibility and diversity of services, pages, or objects to meet the unique requirements of many patrons. These ideas were repeated frequently because they are vital to our collective ability to adapt to change. Regardless of which technologies arise, which industries are disrupted, or how ideas become packaged in the future, librarians will need to carefully allocate resources based on their assessment of users' needs, identify and enhance their own capabilities, design and implement services, promote those services, and then examine what worked well so they can make improvements.

This approach to practice is one that is far too easy to neglect when resources are plentiful and the stakes are low. According to a recent report from the Babson Research Group, over 6.3 million students in the United States took at least one course online from a college or university in 2016 (Seaman, Allen, & Seaman, 2018). This was a 5.6-percent increase from the previous year. Both the trends toward more needs from online users and fewer resources for libraries to meet those needs are likely to continue apace. And, therefore, we expect that it will become vital for all of us to widely adopt best practice. We encourage you to return to the discussions of instructional design, universal design, the ADDIE model, user-centered design, and user-needs assessment, usability, evaluation, and assessment that occur throughout this book.

And while not as concrete as the design approach we advance, we expect that our emphasis on the importance of proactive advocacy is just as practical, perhaps more so. While skill, knowledge, and experience are vital to our ability to serve our online patrons—they are of little use without the will and drive to improve the experiences and opportunities available to them. If we wish to maximize benefits to our online users, we will need to closely follow legal developments pertaining to net neutrality, copyright law, and patron privacy and support approaches that do not make it exorbitantly expensive for libraries to extend resources and access to their entire populations. If publishers of scholarly journals continue to raise prices at rates several times greater than inflation, those among us who want to ensure that high-quality information is available to all citizens will need to encourage open access for information produced for the public good. If shipping prices continue to rise and our patron populations continue to become more geographically dispersed, we will need to advocate for print on demand, or purchase on demand delivery models.

Whatever the challenges of the present or the future, we believe strongly that librarians will be working hard to ensure that patrons will have the freedom and the resources to access the world's information and obtain guidance from someone who values equity and intellectual freedom. And we hope that this volume will contribute to those efforts in ways we cannot yet begin to imagine.

Additional Resources

The following materials are offered as a starting place for additional resources and learning opportunities to help you better serve your online users. This is not an exhaustive list. Rather, we offer it as a means to further dive into the nuances and details of this work. Large organizations like the American Library Association (ALA), Association of College and Research Libraries (ACRL), or the Public Library Association (PLA) will have useful content. The resources on this list have a more specialized focus.

Organizations

- **Code4lib**: Group focused on development and technical aspects of library service. | https://code4lib.org/
- **Distance Learning Section (DLS)** of the ACRL: The premier organization for online learning for libraries in higher education. | http://www.ala.org/acrl/aboutacrl/directoryofleadership/sections/dls/acr-dlsec
- **Emerging Technologies Section (ETS)** of the Reference and User Services Association (RUSA): "Our vision is to equip public-service librarians to implement tech-savvy solutions that improve user experience and library success." | http://www.ala.org/rusa/sections/ets
- **Library Information Technology Association (LITA)**: LITA is concerned with the planning, development, design, application, and integration of technologies within the library and information environment, with the impact of emerging technologies on library service, and with the effect of automated technologies on people. | http://www.ala.org/lita/
- **Library Marketing and Outreach Interest Group**: From the ACRL. Also has a listserv. | http://www.ala.org/acrl/aboutacrl/directoryofleadership/interestgroups/acr-iglmo
- **Marketing and Communications Community of Practice** of the Library Leadership and Management Association (LLAMA) of the ALA: For "those interested and involved in a variety of marketing and communications areas within . . . libraries, including public relations, promotion, content creation,

design, branding, websites, social media, and outreach." It also sponsors the PR Xchange awards. | http://www.ala.org/llama/communities/marketing

- **Project Outcome**: Public Library Association support for measuring outcomes and marketing. | https://www.projectoutcome.org
- **Technology Committee of the Public Library Association (PLA)**: Find standards and tools to help improve services in public libraries. | http://www.ala.org/pla/about/people/committees/pla-tech

Listservs

- **Distance Learning Section of ACRL**: List available only to members of the Distance Learning Section. | dls-l@lists.ala.org
- **LIBREF-L**: Discussion of library reference issues. | https://listserv.kent.edu/cgi-bin/wa.exe?A0=LIBREF-L
- **WCET** (Western Interstate Commission on Higher Education): News and discussion lists for member institutions. | https://wcet.wiche.edu/
- **Web4Lib**: Group focused on servers, services, and applications pertaining to the web. | http://web4lib.org/

Conferences

- **Computers in Libraries**: Conference for librarians focused on general web technologies and applications. | http://computersinlibraries.infotoday.com/2019/Default.aspx
- **Distance Teaching and Learning Conference (DT&L)**: Annual education conference focused on teaching and learning for distance students. | https://dtlconference.wisc.edu
- **Electronic Resources and Libraries (ER&L)**: Conference for librarians focused on electronic resource management, systems, and communications. | https://www.electroniclibrarian.org/conference-info/
- **Library Marketing and Communications Conference**: For library employees of any level involved in marketing, communication, public relations, social media, and outreach. | http://www.librarymarketingconference.org/
- **SIDLIT** (Summer Institute for Distance Learning and Instructional Technology): Low-cost regional conference in the Midwest. Not library focused. | http://blogs.jccc.edu/c2c/sidlit/

Journals

- *Information Technology and Libraries* | https://ejournals.bc.edu/ojs/index.php/ital/index
- *Internet Reference Services Quarterly* | https://www.tandfonline.com/toc/wirs20/current

- *Journal of Library and Information Services in Distance Learning* | https://www.tandfonline.com/loi/wlis20
- *LOEX Quarterly* | https://commons.emich.edu/loexquarterly/
- *Marketing Libraries Journal* | http://journal.marketinglibraries.org/

Standards

- **RUSA Guidelines for Behavioral Performance of Reference and Information Service Providers (2011)** | http://www.ala.org/rusa/resources/guidelines/guidelinesbehavioral
- **Section 508**: GSA IT Accessibility program standards. | https://section508.gov/manage/program-roadmap
- **Standards for Distance Learning Library Services:** Standards created and promoted by the ACRL Distance Learning Section. | http://www.ala.org/acrl/standards/guidelinesdistancelearning

Websites

- **ARS Technica**: General technology site. | https://arstechnica.com/
- **CAST (Center for Applied Special Technology)**: Provides standards and information about universal design for learning. | http://www.cast.org/
- **Circles of Innovation**: Americans with Disabilities Act–compliant video and audio guidelines. | http://circlesofinnovation.valenciacollege.edu/2014/05/23/ada-compliant-video-and-audio-guidelines/
- **EDUCAUSE**: Public policy, education, and technology organization. Publishes horizon reports on libraries and educational organizations. | https://www.educause.edu/
- **Health and Human Services Web Standards**: Guidelines for usability. | https://webstandards.hhs.gov/guidelines/
- **International Federation of Library Associations and Institutions (IFLA) International Marketing Awards** | "Honors organizations that have implemented creative, results-oriented marketing projects or campaigns that promote the library and information services industry." https://www.ifla.org/node/5982
- **Marketing Strategies**: List of marketing resources from the Public Library Association. | http://www.ala.org/pla/resources/tools/public-relations-marketing/marketing-strategies
- **Marketing the Academic Library**: Marketing information from the ACRL. | http://www.ala.org/acrl/issues/marketing
- **PEW Research Center**: Internet and technology research organization. | www.pewinternet.org
- **PRIMO Peer-Reviewed Instructional Materials Online**: Peer-reviewed database of library learning objects. | http://primodb.org/

- **Usability.gov**: Provides a wealth of information about inclusive design. | https://www.usability.gov/
- **Wired**: General technology site. | https://www.wired.com

Software

Usability testing and monitoring:

- **AMP (Accelerated Mobile Pages)**: Open source code library. | https://www.ampproject.org/
- **Crazy Egg**: Paid heat map service. | https://www.crazyegg.com
- **Google Analytics**: Free page-level analytics service. | https://analytics.google.com
- **Screencast-O-Matic**: Free screen recording service. | https://screencast-o-matic.com/
- **WAVE**: Accessibility evaluation tool created by WebAIM. | https://wave.webaim.org/

Research guides:

- **Guide on the Side**: Free library guide service from University of Arizona. | https://ualibraries.github.io/Guide-on-the-Side/
- **LibGuides**: Springshare product with institutional pricing. | https://www.springshare.com/libguides/
- **New Literacies Alliance**: Free curriculum development resources for libraries. | www.newliteraciesalliance.org

Glossary

ADDIE: An instructional design framework that includes the phases of **A**nalysis, **D**esign, **D**evelopment, **I**mplementation, and **E**valuation.

Asynchronous: An environment where a library patron can access and use services during times which library staff are not actively staffing or monitoring the service. May also be referred to as self-paced; students are able to complete assignments without having to be in a specific place or time for class.

Content Management System (CMS): Software that allows you to add and manage content on a website.

Course Guide: A webpage created for a specific class. Can include information about the research assignment, tutorials, and resource lists. Springshare's LibGuide platform is commonly used for course pages, but they can also be created in some learning management systems.

Embed Code: The HTML code that allows you to put a video within a website. This code is generated by popular video sharing sites, including YouTube, and is often found under the "share" link.

Embedded Librarian: A librarian who is integrated in a course in the learning management system. They are not the instructor of the course; rather, they deliver library-related content and guide students through the research process. "Embedded" implies more time and effort than a simple one-shot session.

Information Overload: When a student is presented with too much information at once, they may reduce decision making, tune out, or feel stressed. This happens often online and can easily happen if you try to pack too much information into a short tutorial.

Learning Management System (LMS): The software package that delivers courses to students. In online courses, the LMS is the primary way that content, discussions, and exams are delivered. Some examples include Blackboard, Canvas, and Moodle.

Market Research: Investigating your current and potential patron population in order to make decisions that affect your relationship with them. Can be primary (asking patrons and potential patrons directly) or secondary (utilizing existing data such as census reports).

Mediated Environment: Online interactions that are actively facilitated by a library staff member in real time.

Point-of-Need Instruction: Instruction delivered when the students are ready to use it; that is, they've been introduced to their assignment and have topics in mind. "Point-of-Need" can also refer to tutorials or research guides designed for students to discover on the library's website when they need research help.

Research Guides: Also called "Subject Guides." Include lists of subject-specific resources, including databases and journal collections, eBooks, and print materials. Useful for online patron instruction and can be used to augment lesson plans or reference interactions.

Synchronous: Students are required to attend class online at a specific time. Web conferencing software is often used so that the instructor can lecture and run online classroom activities in real time.

Tutorials: A short explanation of a library-related subject that a student can do at their own pace. Tutorials can include videos, screenshots, and text. Tutorials can have built-in questionnaires and quizzes to make them more interactive for students.

Universal Design: The practice of designing environments for people with a wide variety of circumstances, including differing physical and cognitive abilities.

Usability Study: Testing a product, application, or online environment with users representative of the target audience.

User-Centered Design: Design based on an explicit understanding of users, tasks, and environments (https://www.usability.gov/).

References

American Library Association. (2008). *Definitions of reference*. Retrieved from http://www.ala.org/rusa/guidelines/definitionsreference

American Library Association. (2009). *Access to digital information, services, and networks: An interpretation of the Library Bill of Rights*. Retrieved from http://www.ala.org/advocacy/intfreedom/librarybill/interpretations/accessdigital

American Library Association. (2011). *Guidelines for the behavioral performance of reference and information service providers*. Retrieved from http://www.ala.org/rusa/resources/guidelines/guidelinesbehavioral

American Library Association. (2013). *Information literacy competency standards for nursing*. Retrieved from http://www.ala.org/acrl/standards/nursing

American Library Association. (2015). *Framework for Information Literacy for Higher Education*. Retrieved from http://www.ala.org/acrl/standards/ilframework

American Library Association. (2016). *Standards for distance learning library services*. Retrieved from http://www.ala.org/acrl/standards/guidelinesdistancelearning

American Library Association. (2017). *Guidelines for implementing and maintaining virtual reference services*. Retrieved from http://www.ala.org/rusa/sites/ala.org.rusa/files/content/GuidelinesVirtualReference_2017.pdf

Anderson, M., & Perrin, A. (2017). *Tech adoption climbs among older adults*. Retrieved from http://www.pewinternet.org/2017/05/17/tech-adoption-climbs-among-older-adults/

Arinto, P. B. (2013). A framework for developing competencies in open and distance learning. *International Review of Research in Open & Distance Learning, 14*(1), 167–185. Retrieved from http://www.irrodl.org/index.php/irrodl/article/view/1393

Association of Research Libraries. (n.d.). *About LibQUAL+*. Retrieved from http://www.libqual.org/about/about_lq

Average estimated share of library-materials budget spent on digital and print at 4-year public and private nonprofit colleges, 2010–16. (2017, August 18). *The Chronicle of Higher Education*, p. 63.

Baker, A. (2014). Students' preferences regarding four characteristics of information literacy screencasts. *Journal of Library & Information Services in Distance Learning, 8*(1–2), 67–80. https://doi.org/10.1080/1533290X.2014.916247

Bell, H. H., Andrews, D. H., & Wulfeck, W. H., II. (2009). Behavioral task analysis. In K. H. Silber & W. R. Foshay (Eds.), *Handbook of improving performance in the workplace, volume one: Instruction design and training delivery* (pp. 184–226). Hoboken, NJ: John Wiley & Sons. Retrieved from https://doi.org/10.1002/9780470592663.ch6

Bell, S. J., & Shank, J. D. (2007). *Academic librarianship by design: A blended librarian's guide to the tools and techniques.* Chicago, IL: American Library Association.

Block, J. (2008). Distance education library services assessment. *Electronic Journal of Academic and Special Librarianship, 9*(3). Retrieved from http://southernlibrarianship.icaap.org/content/v09n03/block_j01.html

Bonella, L., Pitts, J., & Coleman, J. (2017). How do we market to distance populations, and does it work?: Results from a longitudinal study and a survey of the profession. *Journal of Library Administration, 57*(1), 69–86. https://doi.org/10.1080/01930826.2016.1202720

Breeding, M. (2015). *The future of library resource discovery.* Baltimore, MD: NISO. Retrieved from https://groups.niso.org/apps/group_public/download.php/14487/future_library_resource_discovery.pdf

Bringolf, J. (2008). Universal design: Is it accessible? *Multi: The RIT Journal of Plurality and Diversity in Design, 1*(2), 45–52.

Buck, S. (2011). *Library services for the distance learner: A library needs assessment at Oregon State University.* Paper presented at the 27th Annual Conference on Distance Teaching & Learning, Madison, WI. Retrieved from https://docplayer.net/8772284-Library-services-for-the-distance-learner-a-library-needs-assessment-at-oregon-state-university.html

Cannady, R. E., Fagerheim, B., Williams, B. F., & Steiner, H. (2013). Diving into distance learning librarianship: Tips and advice for new and seasoned professionals. *College & Research Libraries News, 74*(5), 254–261. https://doi.org/10.5860/crln.74.5.8948

Carlson, J., & Kneale, R. (2011). Embedded librarianship in the research context: Navigating new waters. *College & Research Libraries News, 72*(3), 167–170. Retrieved from https://crln.acrl.org/index.php/crlnews/article/view/8530/8848

The Center for Universal Design, North Carolina State University. (1997). *The principles of universal design (Version 2.0).* Retrieved from https://projects.ncsu.edu/design/cud/about_ud/udprinciplestext.htm

Clark, S., & Chinburg, S. (2010). Research performance in undergraduates receiving face to face versus online library instruction: A citation analysis. *Journal of Library Administration, 50*(5–6), 530–542. https://doi.org/10.1080/01930826.2010.488599

Corbett, A., & Brown, A. (2015). The roles that librarians and libraries play in distance education settings. *Online Journal of Distance Learning Administration, 18*(2). Retrieved from https://www.westga.edu/~distance/ojdla/summer182/corbett_brown182.html

Crowley, C. H. (1990, November 27). Bedtime stories told all day long. *The Christian Science Monitor.* Retrieved from https://www.csmonitor.com/1990/1127/pdial.html

Distance Learning Section. Association of College & Research Libraries. (2017). *Tools for online learning* [webcast]. Retrieved from https://drive.google.com/open?id=0BxQDYlcTaXNIdTlJNC1pLVBSdDA

Doran, G. T. (1981). There's a SMART way to write management's goals and objectives. *Management Review, 70*(11), 35–36.

Estabrook, L., Witt, E., & Rainie, L. (2017). *Information searches that solve problems.* Retrieved from https://www.pewinternet.org/wp-content/uploads/sites/9/media/Files/Reports/2007/Pew_UI_LibrariesReport.pdf.pdf

Gilchrist, D. (2015, December 10). *Learning outcomes: From the big picture to the classroom* [Webinar]. Retrieved from: https://www.carli.illinois.edu/products-services/pub-serv/instruction/LearningOutcomes-Gilchrist

Hebert, A. (2016). Hunting and gathering: Attempting to assess services to distance learning students. *Journal of Library & Information Services in Distance Learning, 10*(3–4), 268–276. https://doi.org/10.1080/1533290X.2016.1219203

Holloway, K. (2011). Outreach to distance students: A case study of a new distance librarian. *Journal of Library & Information Services in Distance Learning, 5*(1–2), 25–33. https://doi.org/10.1080/1533290X.2011.548231

Horton, W. (2011). *E-learning by design* (2nd ed.). Hoboken, NJ: Wiley & Sons. Retrieved from https://onlinelibrary.wiley.com/doi/10.1002/9781118256039.ch2

Huwiler, A. G. (2015). Library services for distance students: Opportunities and challenges. *Journal of Library & Information Services in Distance Learning, 9*(4), 275–288. https://doi.org/10.1080/1533290X.2015.1111283

IBM. (2017). *10 key marketing trends for 2017 and ideas for exceeding customer expectations.* Retrieved from https://public.dhe.ibm.com/common/ssi/ecm/wr/en/wrl12345usen/watson-customer-engagement-watson-marketing-wr-other-papers-and-reports-wrl12345usen-20170719.pdf

Jerabek, J. A., McMain, L. M., & Van Roekel, J. L. (2002). Using needs assessment to determine library services for distance learning programs. *Journal of Interlibrary Loan, Document Delivery & Information Supply, 12*(4), 41–61. https://doi.org/10.1300/J110v12n04_06

Johnson, M., Clapp, M. J., Ewing, S. R., & Buhler, A. G. (2011). Building a participatory culture: Collaborating with student organizations for twenty-first century library instruction. *Collaborative Librarianship, 3*(1), 2–15. Retrieved from https://digitalcommons.du.edu/collaborativelibrarianship/vol3/iss1/2

Joo, S., & Choi, N. (2016). Understanding users' continuance intention to use online library resources based on an extended expectation-confirmation model. *The Electronic Library, 34*(4), 554–571. https://doi.org/10.1108/EL-02-2015-0033

Larson, J. (2012). *CREW: A weeding manual for modern libraries.* Austin, TX: The Texas State Library. Retrieved from https://www.tsl.texas.gov/sites/default/files/public/tslac/ld/ld/pubs/crew/crewmethod12.pdf

Lemley, T. (2016). Virtual embedded librarianship program: A personal view. *Journal of the Medical Library Association: JMLA, 104*(3), 232–234. https://doi.org/10.3163/1536-5050.104.3.010

Lowe, M. S., Booth, C., & Savova, M. (2014). *Claremont Colleges library faculty library survey summary report: 2014.* Retrieved from http://scholarship.claremont.edu/library_staff/24

Marcum, B. (2016). Embracing change: Adapting and evolving your distance learning library services to meet the new ACRL Distance Learning Library Services Standards. *Journal of Library & Information Services in Distance Learning, 10*(3–4), 332–339. https://doi.org/10.1080/1533290X.2016.1221625

Martin, N., & Martin, R. (2014). *Would you watch it? Creating effective & engaging video tutorials* [Webinar]. Retrieved from http://blendedlibrarian.learningtimes.net/would-you-watch-it-creating-effective-and-engaging-video-tutorials/#.VDfd_tTF800

McLean, E., & Dew, S. H. (2004). Assessing the library needs and preferences of off-campus students. *Journal of Library Administration, 41*(1–2), 265–302. https://doi.org/10.1300/J111v41n01_20

Oakleaf, M. (2009). The information literacy instruction assessment cycle: A guide for increasing student learning and improving librarian instructional skills. *Journal of Documentation, 65*(4), 539–560. https://doi.org/10.1108/00220410910970249

O'Kelly, M. (2015). Seven questions for assessment planning: A discussion starter. *College & Research Libraries News, 76*(9), 488–494. Retrieved from https://crln.acrl.org/index.php/crlnews/article/view/9380/10548

Pagowsky, N., & McElroy, K. (Eds.). (2016). *Critical library pedagogy handbook.* Chicago, IL: Association of College and Research Libraries.

Pitts, J., Coleman, J., & Bonella, L. (2013). Using distance patron data to improve library services and cross-campus collaboration. *Internet Reference Services Quarterly, 18*(1), 55–75. https://doi.org/10.1080/10875301.2013.800014

Project Outcome. (2019). *About Project Outcome.* Retrieved from https://www.projectoutcome.org/about

Roth, A., & Turnbow, D. (2016, June 9). *Walking the path together: Creating an instructional design team to elevate learning.* Presentation at Library Instruction West, Salt Lake City, UT. Retrieved from http://digitalcommons.usu.edu/cgi/viewcontent.cgi?article=1006&context=liw16

Seaman, J. E., Allen, I. E., & Seaman, J. (2018). *Grade increase: Tracking distance education in the United States.* Retrieved from https://onlinelearningsurvey.com/reports/gradeincrease.pdf

Seel, N. M., Lehmann, T., Blumschein, P., & Podolskiy, O. A. (2017). *Instructional design for learning: Theoretical foundations.* Rotterdam, The Netherlands: Sense Publishers.

Shumaker, D., & Talley, M. (2009). *Models of embedded librarianship: Final report.* Retrieved from https://embeddedlibrarian.files.wordpress.com/2013/04/models-of-embedded-librarianship_finalreportrev.pdf

Steinfeld, E., & Maisel, J. (2012). *Universal design: Creating inclusive environments.* Hoboken, NJ: John Wiley & Sons.

Tang, Y. (2013). Distance education librarians in the United States: A study of job announcements. *The Journal of Academic Librarianship, 39*(6), 500–505. https://doi.org/10.1016/j.acalib.2013.08.012

University of the West Indies. (n.d.). *The UWI triple a strategy 2017–2022: Revitalizing Caribbean development.* Retrieved from https://sta.uwi.edu/fss/heu/sites/default/files/heu/The%20UWI%20Triple%20A%20Strategic%20Plan%202017%20-%202022%20Full%20Plan%20.pdf

U.S. Department of Education. (n.d.). *Higher Education Opportunity Act—2008.* Retrieved from https://www2.ed.gov/policy/highered/leg/hea08/index.html

U.S. Department of Education, Office of Postsecondary Education. (n.d.). *FAQ about accreditation.* Retrieved from https://ope.ed.gov/accreditation/FAQAccr.aspx

U.S. Department of Health and Human Services. (n.d.). *User-centered design basics.* Retrieved from https://www.usability.gov/what-and-why/user-centered-design.html

U.S. Department of Justice. (n.d.). *The Americans with Disabilities Act of 1990 and revised ADA regulations implementing Title II and Title III.* Retrieved from https://www.ada.gov/2010_regs.htm

Vai, M., & Sosulski, K. (2011). *Essentials of online course design: A standards-based guide.* New York, NY: Routledge.

Wharton, L. N. (2017). From assessment to implementation: Using qualitative interviews to inform distance learning library services. *Journal of Library & Information Services in Distance Learning, 11*(1–2), 196–205. https://doi.org/10.1080/1533290X.2016.1232051

Wiggins, G. P., & McTighe, J. (2005). *Understanding by design* (2nd ed.). Alexandria, VA: Association for Supervision and Curriculum Development.

About the Editors and Contributors

Karla Aleman is the dean of the Library and eLearning Division at Lorain County Community College in Elyria, Ohio. She has spent the past three years leading campus initiatives in digital learning, electronic accessibility, equity, and student learning strategic planning. She also leads the library's award-winning partnership with the Elyria Public Library System in offering joint collections and programming to the campus and greater community. Previously, Karla served as the distance instruction librarian at Morehead State University in Morehead, Kentucky. While at Morehead State University, her scholarship explored services to rural populations and stimulating student engagement through the use of animated GIFs and other web technologies. Before Morehead State University, Karla was a faculty librarian at the College of DuPage, a community college in Glen Ellyn, Illinois.

Laura Bonella is an academic services librarian and associate professor at Kansas State University Libraries. In addition to her responsibilities supporting students and faculty in education and social sciences as the team lead of the libraries' social sciences/education/business team, she serves on the libraries' distance education team. She has chaired the ACRL Women and Gender Studies Section (ACRL/WGSS) and multiple committees in ACRL/WGSS and the ACRL Education and Behavioral Sciences Section. She serves as the convener of the ACRL Balancing Baby and Book discussion group. In 2019, she began a three-year term as an ALA councillor at large. Her research interests include services and marketing to distance education patrons and how academics select journals for publication. She has published and presented over 25 times on these topics at the local, regional, and national levels.

Stefanie Buck worked for Oregon State University Libraries from 2009 to 2019 as the Ecampus librarian. In this role, she assisted students from all over the world in conducting research and accessing library resources remotely. As of March 2019, Stefanie is the director of Open Educational Resources (OER), a unit within Oregon State's Ecampus division that focuses on affordable learning through no- and low-cost course materials. Stefanie has served as the chair of the Association of College and Research Libraries' Distance Learning Section. Stefanie's research interests include learning analytics, OER discoverability, and student success with open educational resources.

Jason M. Coleman is head of the Library User Services Department and associate professor at Kansas State University Libraries. In that role he is responsible for circulation, reserves, and general reference services at three libraries. He also serves on the libraries' distance education team and manages the libraries' IM chat service. In 2016 he received the libraries' Brice G. Hobrock Distinguished Faculty Award. His research interests include critical library instruction, user experience design for discovery services, management of reference services, and identification of factors influencing innovation. He has chaired several national committees in the American Library Association's Reference User Services Association, including ETS' Best Emerging Technology Application Award Committee and the RSS/ETS Virtual Reference Tutorial Committee. Link to CV.

Natalie Haber joined the University of Tennessee at Chattanooga in 2014 as the online services librarian where she implements and promotes innovative online tools and services for both off-campus and on-campus learners. She is also a member of the library instruction team and teaches many classes face to face. Natalie's research interests include information literacy, online learning, user experience, and assessment of online instruction.

Joelle E. Pitts is head of the Content Development Department and associate professor at Kansas State University Libraries. In that role she is responsible for collection development, analysis, and management of print and online materials. She also leads the award-winning New Literacies Alliance, an inter-institutional information literacy consortium dedicated to creating institutional, technological, and vendor-agnostic online lessons. In 2014 she received the Libraries' Brice G. Hobrock Distinguished Faculty Award. Previously, she served as the instructional design librarian for Kansas State University Libraries. Her research interests include distance education and e-learning theory and design, library collaboration, as well as the intersections of scholarly communication and information literacy. She has published and presented on these topics at the local, national, and international levels.

Elaine Sullo is the coordinator of Information and Instructional Services at the George Washington University's Himmelfarb Health Sciences Library. She is the library liaison to the School of Nursing, where she provides instruction to undergraduate- and graduate-level nursing students, as well as online support as the embedded librarian to distance education students. She has collaborated on systematic reviews with medicine and nursing faculty and is an evidence summary writer for the online journal *Evidence Based Library & Information Practice*.

Adam Wathen is the associate director for Systemwide Services at Johnson County Library in Overland Park, Kansas. He oversees the programming, outreach, collection, technical services, and circulation of Johnson County Library. He has formerly acted as a collection manager at Johnson County Library and in academic libraries in roles as a reference librarian, government publications librarian, acquisitions manager, and director of a private college library.

Index

Page numbers followed by *f* or *t* indicate figures or tables, respectively.